DEATH AND GRIEF IN THE FAMILY

James C. Hansen, Editor
Thomas T. Frantz, Volume Editor

The Family Therapy Collections

AN ASPEN PUBLICATION®

Aspen Systems Corporation
Rockville, Maryland
Royal Tunbridge Wells
1984

Library of Congress Cataloging in Publication Data
Main entry under title:

Death and grief in the family.

(The Family therapy collections, ISSN 0735-9152; 8)
Includes index.
Contents: Unfinished business/Elisabeth Kubler-Ross—
Parents whose child has died/Thomas T. Frantz—Helping
the partner of the cancer patient/Betty Satterwhite-
Stevenson—[etc.]
1. Death—Psychological aspects—Addresses, essays, lectures.
2. Bereavement—Psychological aspects—Addresses, essays,
lectures. 3. Family—Psychological aspects—Addresses, essays,
lectures. I. Hansen, James C. II. Series.
BF789.D4D36   1984   155.9'37   83-21430
ISBN 0-89443-608-2

The Family Therapy Collections series is indexed in
Psychological Abstracts and the PsycINFO database.

The poem that appears on pages 9 and 10 is reprinted with
permission from *Living, Loving and Learning* by Leo Buscaglia,
© Leo Buscaglia.

Publisher: John Marozsan
Editorial Director: Margaret Quinlin
Executive Managing Editor: Margot Raphael
Editorial Services: Ruth Judy
Printing and Manufacturing: Debbie Collins

Library of Congress Catalog Card Number: 83-21430
ISBN: 0-89433-608-2
ISSN: 0735-9152

Printed in the United States of America

1 2 3 4 5

Table of Contents

Board of Editors

Board of Editors

(continued)

Contributors

THOMAS T. FRANTZ
State University of New York
Buffalo, New York

SANDRA BERTMAN
University of Massachusetts
Medical School
Worchester, Massachusetts

ELISABETH KUBLER-ROSS
Shanti Nilaya
Escondido, California

MARCIA E. LATTANZI
Boulder County Hospice
Boulder, Colorado

IRIS BOLTON
The Link Counseling Center
Atlanta, Georgia

J. DONALD SCHUMACHER
Somerville, Massachusetts

BRUCE CONLEY
The Conley Funeral Home
Elburn, Illinois

BETTY SATTERWHITE STEVENSON
University of Rochester
Rochester, New York

RICHARD J. GOLDBERG
Brown University Hospital
Providence, Rhode Island

ROBERT M. TULL
Kaiser-Permanente Medical Center
Hayward, California

Preface

The Family Therapy Collections, published quarterly, are designed primarily for practicing professionals. Each volume contains articles authored by professional practitioners, providing in-depth coverage of a single significant topic in family therapy.

This volume focuses on death in a family. In our culture, most people die outside their homes, usually in a hospital. Much of the reality of death is lost when the family cannot share in the experience of the death process, and this may affect the process of grieving. The death of a family member is a loss that affects the other members' social and mental-emotional identities. Mourning involves a series of reactions that enable a bereaved person to repair the social disruption and reinforce emotional ties with other family members. Grief therapy has found its way into this problematic area to help individuals deal with their thoughts and feelings throughout this process. Grief therapy is designed to forestall the pathological developments that can follow bereavement.

Family therapists may be called upon to assist families in crisis immediately after a death, or families that present symptoms much later. The articles in this volume will help family therapists understand the grief process and the impact dying and death can have on family members. While grief therapy has focused primarily on individuals, family therapists can use these insights to work with whole families or subsystems. Knowledge of the grief process and working with grief can also assist family therapists in understanding and working with symptoms that appear later in a family.

Dr. Thomas T. Frantz is the volume editor. Dr. Frantz is an Associate Professor of Counseling and Educational Psychology at the State University of New York at Buffalo. He is the founder of the Life and Death Transition

Center, a United Way agency that provides in-service training, counseling, and information about coping with grief and terminal illness; co-founder of the seven Western New York Chapters of Compassionate Friends (self-help and support groups for bereaved parents); founder of the Suicide Bereavement Group; and co-founder of the Western New York Chapter of Parents of Murdered Children. He is the psychological consultant to Hospice Buffalo; on the board of directors of the Sudden Infant Death parents group, the South Buffalo Grief Center, and the American Cancer Society's support and visitation program for cancer patients; and is the director of the Cancer Care Program, a self-help and therapy program for cancer patients and their families.

James C. Hansen
Editor

Introduction

We in the 1980s are treading gingerly, but with increasing confidence, amidst the reverberations of three revolutions launched in the decade of the 1970s. As with many revolutions, the ideas were not new but the rapidity with which they spread through post-Vietnam society was.

First, Elisabeth Kubler-Ross opened the door to let death and dying out of the closet where nursing homes, hospitals, and modern medicine had hidden them for much of our century. The publication of her book, *On Death and Dying*, in 1969 marked the beginning of dying, cancer, grief, suicide, and death appearing regularly in our newspapers, magazines, books, television talk shows, and radio interviews. Death generates much fear and therefore much resistance, yet increasing numbers of people (though probably still a minority) are able to think about it, discuss it, and reach out to others affected by its anticipation and aftermath.

Second, systems theory emerged from biology to permeate the technological and social sciences. It created a new paradigm through which phenomena previously viewed as individual began to be studied and treated as parts of an interacting system. The infusion of systems approaches into the study and counseling of families helped revitalize family therapy to the point where theory with an increasing number of clients—especially children, adolescents, and cancer patients—is undertaken only with the client's family involved in the therapeutic process. Family theory has become a major treatment approach.

Third, self-help and support groups following the prototype of Alcoholics Anonymous (AA) are being formed in ever-increasing numbers. Led usually by untrained group members, people are meeting in groups to help each other cope with problems like cancer, diabetes, scleredema, ostomies, murdered children, widowhood, open heart surgery, and suicide. For example, in the spring of 1978 our Compassionate Friends chapter in Buffalo was one of but a handful of chapters nationwide. Now there are a dozen chapters in Western New York and close to 400 nationwide.

All three revolutions arise, I think, from the same source: mobility destroying the homestead and the extended family. The average family moves every seven years and approximately 20 to 25 percent of Americans move every year. The family home used to be the hospital, nursing home, and funeral parlor as well as a place of dependable security to family members as they grew up. Members of the extended family were the nurses, baby sitters, social workers, and counselors. But this is no longer typical.

The three societal changes to which I refer reflect the demise of old family homes and communities of extended families. Family therapists are right in the middle of these changes. Our discipline is deeply involved in them; unresolved grief over death or other losses can be seen as the root of a majority of our clients' problems, and people reaching out for extended family substitutes demonstrates the importance of attending to family systems.

This volume of *The Family Therapy Collections* brings the experiences of those who work with death and grief to an audience of therapists who work with families. The volume reflects the early developmental state of grief counseling, in that most grief counselors work primarily with individuals and, more specifically, with individuals in acute phases of dying or grieving. In reading the articles that follow you will often need to make adaptations in applying the background, ideas, and suggestions that are offered.

The lady to whom dying and grieving people owe so much, Elisabeth Kubler-Ross, begins our volume in her wonderful free-spirited style by speaking to us more as people than professionals about how finishing our unfinished business, and helping others do the same, can prevent so much grief work and tragedy. She makes a distinction between grief—which is normal, healthy, and should be encouraged—and grief work, which arises from unfinished business.

Anna, in *The King and I*, teaches "by your pupils you'll be taught." The second article reflects this wisdom, as it contains a translation of experiences and testimonies from hundreds of meetings with bereaved parents. I've tried to express the reactions parents experience following their child's death and also to convey what grieving parents found helpful.

Betty Satterwhite-Stevenson treats the seldom addressed problem of helping the spouse or partner of a cancer patient. Her writing flows from her unique combination of professional experiences with families at the University of Rochester Medical School and personal experiences as the wife of a man who died of cancer and as a cancer patient herself.

The third of the three articles focusing on adults reflects Iris Bolton's experience with her son's suicide and her work with individuals and families as director of the Link Counseling Center in Atlanta, Georgia. She emphasizes the need for postvention with surviving family members following a suicide, pointing out that the effect of a person killing himself may ultimately be as destructive to other family members as the suicide was to the suicide victim.

In the first of four articles examining the effects of death in the family on children, Sandra Bertman of the University of Massachusetts Center for Medical Humanities discusses the value of examining children's drawings for clues to their feelings about death and dying. The reactions of teenagers, particularly around the time immediately following a death, are discussed by Bruce Conley, a funeral director in Elburn, Illinois. Bruce writes from a vantage point most of us only hear about weeks or months after the death.

Bob Tull has been working in hospitals in Buffalo, New York; Providence, Rhode Island; and Berkeley, California with children who have cancer and the families of young people with cancer for seven years. He shows that many other concerns—their changing role in the family, body image, and peer group acceptance—become paramount for children and adolescents as they try to live with cancer.

In the last article on children, Don Schumacher reviews the literature on the effects of a child's death on the surviving siblings and concludes that children often grieve alone while parents get the attention. Chairman of the board of a suburban Boston Hospice, Don has worked with children and families in hospitals and through his private practice in the Boston area.

Many of us who work with dying and grieving people soon discover the unfinished business it awakens in us. Unresolved grief, fear of losing people we love, and feelings of powerlessness may surface. In the volume's final article, Maria Lattanzi deals with ways of coping with the effects our work has on us. In her work with Colorado's Boulder County Hospice she has had ample experience with the stresses our work produces and she concludes that we need each other for the very reasons our clients need us: to listen, to grieve, and to know that we are not alone.

Thomas T. Frantz
Volume Editor

1. Unfinished Business

Elisabeth Kubler-Ross, M.D.
Shanti Nilaya
Escondido, California

ALTHOUGH THEY MAY NOT RECOGNIZE IT INTELLECTUALLY, HUMAN beings are aware of their own impending death, whether it is a homicide, a suicide, a sudden death, or a slow natural death. If we would pay close attention, we could eliminate the grief work of our society—not grief, but grief work. Grief is a very natural emotion; it is really a God-given gift that allows us to come to grips with any loss in life, whether it is the loss of a valued item or a death in the family. It is not necessary to work with grief; it involves shedding tears, sharing, and talking, but it will heal. Grief work, in contrast, is shame, guilt, and fear ("Oh, my God if I had only done this or that!"). The real grief work should be done before tragedy strikes.

My big hope is that we raise a generation of children who learn about their natural emotions in such a way that they have no grief work. Then, if a tragedy happens, they will go through natural grief; but they will not need a psychiatrist, Valium, or counseling. They will be able to look back over their lives and bless those tragedies later on in life, because they will know that, if it had not been for those tragedies, they would never have become who they are today. Windstorms make the beautiful carvings on the canyon walls.

In the last 10 years, I have worked mainly with dying children, with parents of murdered children, and with parents whose children committed suicide. One family in San Francisco lost all their children to cancer in less than a year. One mother, a single mother in Indianapolis, went to get some milk; when she came back, her three sons were lying on the living room floor on their bellies, dead, having been shot in the neck gangland style. Another single mother had three children who committed suicide in 2 years! They were an apparently average American middle-class family, and there had been no drug abuse and no big tragedies. A mother who already lives alone and loses one child after another to suicide must feel that she is going insane.

The United States is the most blessed, richest country in the world. Yet 1 million American children run away from home every year, and 10,000 are murdered. Thousands end up as 13- or 14-year-old prostitutes from San Francisco to Tokyo. Suicide is the third leading cause of death of children between the ages of 6 and 16. No country has more tragedies with their healthy, beautiful children than does America. In order to prevent the grief work associated with such tragedies, we must all have the courage, the honesty, the humility, and the integrity to examine our own lives from the inside, especially our unfinished business. Whatever we have not finished in our lives will be passed on as unfinished business to our children. If we manage our own lives well, we will be able to raise a generation of children

2

who will be whole; they will experience their physical, emotional, intellectual, and spiritual selves as one.

Physicians used to take care only of physical problems. Now it is becoming clearer and clearer that emotional problems contribute to health. Physicians are more honest with patients and try to satisfy their intellectual curiosity.

If people learn again to balance the physical, emotional, intellectual, and spiritual parts of themselves, they will become natural again and will begin to discover that they are very, very intuitive, very spiritual. The whole person is so intuitive that he or she is always at the right place at the right time. All things happen when the time is right, and there is no unfinished business.

I was at the San Francisco airport. I had lectured for 3 days, I was tired, I was dying to get home; and my plane was standing there. I had only one day at home before I was to leave for Europe. Thinking about home and packing for Europe, I had already tuned out the people around me when a woman pulled my blouse and said, "Dr. Ross." I wanted to say "No, my name is Mary Smith." The woman instantly knew that I wanted to be left alone, but she said, "I really need help. In October, we lost our 9-year-old boy. Two weeks after his funeral, we were told that our 11-year-old daughter was full of cancer. We cannot take anymore . . . we can't even go into her bedroom. I'm beginning to resent her . . . I just can't cope with her . . . we really, really need help." I really wanted to help this family, but I knew that my plane was leaving in 5 minutes, that I had to get home, that I had to do my laundry and repack for Europe, etc. All I said to myself was, "Oh, my God, if I only had one hour, right here, right now, that's really all I would need." Thirty seconds later, it was announced over the loudspeaker that "Flight 83 is delayed by one hour." My whole life is like this. If I am not getting somewhere, I know I am not supposed to be there; sometimes, weeks later, I understand why.

If these things happen day after day after day, one learns not to worry about tomorrow, but to do what can be done today. Because this state of mind eliminates fears, anxieties, and worries, more energy can be directed toward what must be done today. It is important that therapists learn to live this way. Therapists waste too much energy on worrying. If they do their own inner homework, they will be so tuned into patients that they do not need textbooks. By listening to what each person says at a given moment, the therapist will know exactly what to do, what the patient needs, and how to help that person. Therapists who have unfinished business of their own, however, are unlikely to hear their patients.

THE PHYSICAL SELF

In the first year of a baby's life, physical care is absolutely the most important. Hugging, holding, touching—as much physical contact as possible—gives the babies of our future generation the most healthy basic background to become whole again. This approach is also applicable to families that are hurting, to terminally ill patients, and to all people in nursing homes. The greatest need of terminally ill patients is physical care. Physical care is a very basic thing, but it is sometimes forgotten. Physical care means ensuring that an incontinent patient is clean and dry before bringing a visitor and not tying up old, senile people.

I went to a very good (supposedly) nursing home and found that the old people had been tied into their chairs and were literally hanging in their chairs. I said to one of the nurses, "I can't believe this. This is the United States, 1982." She become very angry with me and said, "Would you rather they slip out of their chairs and break their hips?" I said "Yes." There is something wrong with an existence in which hands are tied to prevent a broken leg. Physical care includes making it possible for the elderly to move, to hold, and to hug.

Every terminally ill patient should be touched, loved, and hugged. When women have breast cancer, their husbands often act as if they have leprosy, moving out of the bedroom and ending their intimate life. When they most need to feel lovable and acceptable, people may be rejected the most. Only when the physical needs of being loved, hugged and touched, and appreciated are met can people become whole, however. This is true of children, old people, parents, dying patients, and any one in-between.

My dream is to establish Gerontology-Toddler centers. Old people in nursing homes and the toddlers of working parents would give each other hugs, smooches, and touching. Old people would not become senile if they could fall in love with a toddler or two who would sit on their laps and give them hugs again. The elderly would find their physical needs met and the young children would grow up loving old wrinkled faces again.

THE EMOTIONAL SELF

God created man so that his physical self is paramount in the first year of life. It is a person's foundation, like the basement of a house. The emotional self develops between ages one and six. This is when the basic attitudes that ruin lives are obtained. Emotional problems as a result of unfinished business are the cause of most of the suicides in the United States, the cause of the filled prisons, the cause of the institutional tragedies.

Fears such as fear of fire, rejection, or failure are unhealthy and totally unnatural. They drain energy and prevent people from being whole. There are only two natural fears, the fear of falling and the fear of sudden loud noises. These are necessary for survival. Therapists who have any other fears must become aware of them and work to eliminate them.

Grief is one of the most important emotions. Its natural expression is tears. Yet, children between the ages of one and six are often told when they cry, "Stop crying!" "Be a big girl." "Big boys don't cry." This prevents children from becoming whole human beings. People who were not allowed to express natural grief as children have problems for the rest of their lives because life consists of thousands of little deaths. Of course, repressed grief does not cause all problems, but it is certainly a contributing factor.

Guilt can be overcome only by sharing it with a group of accepting, unconditionally loving people. If it is shared from the gut, not the head, the patient will be able to shed tears, to grieve, and then to learn self-forgiveness. In sudden death, people often feel a great deal of guilt and shame. A black woman in Chicago who lived in a huge apartment building for poor people was so worn out she just could not take anymore. The family barely survived physically, and she had several children to raise alone. Finally she found a lover and said to herself, "Now my life is going to begin to take shape with a family and a husband."

One day she was exhausted and really needed to be alone with her boy friend for a little while. Her 6-year-old girl ran in and out until the mother lost her patience and screamed at the little girl, "Why don't you get out of my life?" It was just an expression of "I've had it, I just can't take it anymore." The girl ran out screaming and crying. Later, it was found that the child had gone up on the roof of this very tall building. There, three or four boys had brutally raped her and thrown her off the roof to the ground, where she met her premature and lonely death.

This mother almost died of shame, guilt, and horror. She regrets not having taken her daughter in her arms and saying "I'm sorry, honey, but I really need to be alone for a few minutes." People who have had similar experiences relive the nightmare of that moment in our workshops. They grieve, cry, and share all the "shoulds" and "if I had onlys." When they are able to shed their tears and share their grief, which can take hours of time, the love, compassion, and unconditional acceptance of the group allows them to start living again.

Every unnatural emotion is a piece of unfinished business. For example, *anger* expressed in its natural state takes 15 seconds. People who have not been allowed to be angry will become very mean and nasty; will criticize others; will label others; and will blame others because they do not have the courage to look at their own unfinished business. Anger that is not expressed builds up until the individual explodes, and the explosion certainly lasts longer than 15 seconds. Repressed anger is the biggest killer of our society in terms of angry individuals' health and in terms of tragedy. It results in hate and revenge.

All little children are *jealous*. It is a gift, as emulating other children helps them learn to ice skate, to read the alphabet, to play the flute. When grown-ups make it ugly, it turns into envy and competition.

Unconditional love helps keep natural emotions natural and flowing. Most of us were raised on "I love you if"—if you make it through high school, if you bring good grades home, for example. People do things to be loved, to get their parents' approval; they may never become what they want to become. Nine out of ten adults tell me, "Dr. Ross, I made a living, but I never really lived." To me, that is grief work. If they have the courage, people can change that before it is too late. If they do what they love to do, they may have to go through some hardships, but they will be blessed beyond measure.

Unconditional love does not mean always doing things for other people or never saying no. The mother who ties her son's shoelaces until he is 12 years old makes an emotional cripple of this child. He will have no self-respect, no self-trust, and no self-love. A first-grader who wants to go on the school bus may suddenly say "No, Mommy, I want to stay home. I'm not ready." A mother who knows unconditional love will say, "Honey, I know how hard it is the first day of school. It was hard for me, but I'm convinced that you're going to do better than I did. When you come home today, you're going to be so proud." This child will go on the bus and come home feeling very important. That gives a child self-confidence; that is the love that can say no. Therapists who cannot practice this kind of love cannot do good grief counseling.

THE SPIRITUAL SELF

If an individual lives in harmony, the spiritual self develops in adolescence. Many thousands of children die at age 7, 9, 10, however. These children lose physical abilities, but they find something that is better or more significant—they open intuitively and spiritually prematurely. Dying children are all old, wise souls, as they are often called. It is an incredible experience to sit with dying children, and listen to them. They are unusual children who have a compensatory gift that can elevate them into a spiritual plane. Jeffrey was one of these children. He talked like an old, wise man. Shortly before he died, I visited him in the hospital where he had spent most of his life. When I walked into Jeffrey's room, I heard a young eager beaver physician who had just taken over the ward say to Jeffrey's parents, "We're going to try another experimental chemotherapy." He said this very casually, as if it were nothing. If he had looked at Jeffrey, he would have seen the child's face pale and his eyes tear up. He was so fragile, I blurted out, "Did anybody ask Jeffrey?" They shook their heads as if to say you do not ask a 9-year-old child if he wants more treatment. I said, "Yes, you do." He knows what he needs, not from his head, but from his heart.

Those who are not afraid of the answer always ask the patient. Jeffrey's parents loved him unconditionally enough to allow me to ask him in front of them and the doctor what he wanted. Jeffrey looked at me and said, "I don't understand you grown-ups that you have to make us kids so sick to get well." It was very clear, to me at least, that this child knew it was useless to start another experimental chemotherapy. While the grown-ups debated, this little guy who could barely stand said very loud and clear, "No, thank you!" The parents were able to hear it, which is the highest form of love. They said, "O.K., in that case, we will take him home."

I said goodbye to Jeffrey, and he said very matter of factly, "No, you come home with me." I thought about all the patients I had to see; before I said a word, he said, "Don't worry. It only takes 10 minutes." They know and respect limits, and they answer unasked questions. Total connectedness is the wisdom of these children. So, I thought, "10 minutes, I can be with any child." We hopped in the car and drove to typical suburbia.

As we drove into the garage, Jeffrey said to his father, very brief, unsentimental, and to the point, "Take my bicycle down off the wall." There was a bicycle hanging on the wall that his father had bought for him years earlier. He said that the only thing in life that he had not done and wanted to do once in his lifetime was to ride around the block on his beloved bicycle. He had never been able to do it because of his illness. So he asked his father to take that bicycle down and with tears in his eyes—that is humility—he said, "Put the training wheels on."

With tears in his eyes the father put the training wheels on. Then Jeffrey looked at me with a big smirk (dying patients have more humor than grown-ups and healthy people) and said, "You're here to hold my mom back." That was not a joke; he was dead serious. He knew his mother wanted to lift him onto the bicycle, and she would have held him there and run around the block with him.

So, I held his mother back, and his father held me back. The three of us had to hold onto each other to overcome that urge to be overprotective. This little guy was like a drunk man; with absolutely his last ounce of energy, he climbed on that bicycle with training wheels. The only thing we did was to give him a little speed with a little push. It was the longest wait we had until he came around the block. He was grinning as if he had won a gold medal in the Olympics. The triumph—I mean . . . that his biggest wish had been fulfilled. Then, he became again, a typical 9-year-old. He asked his father to take the training wheels off and carry the bicycle upstairs to his bedroom.

Then he looked at me and said, "You can go now." I like that lack of sentimentality. These children do what they need to do. That was the last time I saw Jeffrey. Later that day, Jeff called his brother to his bedroom and told him that he wanted to give him the bicycle now for a birthday present, that he would not be around on his birthday, but that he wanted the pleasure of giving it to his brother himself.

These parents have no grief work, although they have a great deal of grief over the loss of a 9-year-old boy. They would have a fantastic amount of grief work if, because of their own needs, because of their own inability to let go, because of their own lack of unconditional love, they had insisted on another experimental chemotherapy. Jeffrey would have died, probably in an intensive care unit, sick and nauseated, bald and miserable, without having fulfilled his greatest wish.

Until therapists learn that each person makes his or her own choices and lives through the consequences of these choices, they will not help one human being, no matter how many courses about grief they take or how many books they read. Therapists must understand that it is not the years that people live, it is how they have lived. If they live fully, they will feel that they have lived a hundred lives.

A woman came to a lecture I was giving one night. She was what is called a proper lady. She came up to the stage after the lecture, but each time that it had been her turn to speak to me she retreated. This went on until about 11:00 at night, when she gave up and left. The next morning, she came at 6:00 in the morning to my motel room, which is very unladylike. She had heard that I had a plane at 7:00 so she came at the last minute. She gave the greatest gift anybody ever gave me from the audience.

She said, "I have to tell you what happened to me last night." I came home, and there sat my 18-year-old son. He sat on the refrigerator where he sits every night with his friends." The way she used the word *friends* said a great deal. She said, "He wears this gray, washed-out, horrible undefinable tee-shirt that he got from one of his girl friends. I can't stand it. What do the neighbors think—that we can't dress our children right."

"Every time I come home and see him sitting on the refrigerator with his friends and that tee-shirt, I start lashing out at him. That's how we go to bed every night. Last night I came home later than usual, and there he sat again on that refrigerator with his friends. I suddenly looked at him for the first time, and I heard myself say, 'Bob, if you want to wear that tee-shirt it's O.K. with me because tonight, if you drive your friends home in this old car and you have a fatal accident, I would bury you in that tee-shirt.'"

She came to tell me that and to thank me. Why do our children have to die before we appreciate what is important? This is our unfinished business. Our children must do their own growing up and learn their own lessons. Loving a child unconditionally does not mean total permissiveness. Firm, consistent discipline starts and ends between one and six. Once they have learned, parents need not worry. All these piercing words about other people's opinions ruin children's lives. If the proper lady's son had died before that night, she would have spent years doing her grief work with psychiatrists or therapists.

CONCLUSION

My dream is that we spend our energies and love in preventing grief work, not in applying Bandaids when it is, theoretically speaking, too late. That is to me the biggest dream and the biggest hope.

Life is very simple and beautiful. Any human being who holds onto a bad mood does so only for the purpose of punishing God, destiny, the boss, the husband, the wife, the children, the mother-in-law, anything; including himself or herself. It is a waste of energy. The poem, "Things You Didn't Do" puts it well.

Remember the day I borrowed your brand new car and I dented it?
I thought you'd kill me, but you didn't.
And remember the time I dragged you to the beach, and you said it
would rain, and it did?
I thought you'd say, "I told you so." But you didn't.

Do you remember the time I flirted with all the guys to make you jealous, and you were?
I thought you'd leave me, but you didn't.
Do you remember the time I spilled strawberry pie all over your car rug?
I thought you'd hit me, but you didn't.
And remember the time I forgot to tell you the dance was formal and you showed up in jeans?
I thought you'd drop me, but you didn't.
Yes, there were lots of things you didn't do.
But you put up with me, and you loved me, and you protected me.
There were lots of things I wanted to make up to you when you returned from Viet Nam.
But you didn't.

This is unfinished business.

2. Helping Parents Whose Child Has Died

Thomas T. Frantz
State University of New York
Buffalo, New York

PEOPLE HAVE A TENDENCY TO GRIEVE THE LOSS OF SOMEONE THEY love in much the way they have learned to grieve other losses in their life. By the time we become adults, each of us has experienced loss many times. Hence, each of us has developed our own particular coping style, our own way of responding to loss, our own grieving process.

If we are going to be of help to people who are grieving the loss of a loved one, the place to start is by paying attention to our own coping style, our own way of grieving, because we have a natural tendency to expect that other people will grieve in the way we grieve, or to assume that they should grieve in the way that we grieve.

It is very difficult to help somebody that we can't identify with or that we are busy judging. Largely because, even though we may not voice the judgment, the grieving person picks up intuitively, nonverbally, the message of our disapproval, the message of our criticism, the message that we think they're not handling it right. It's not something that's put into words; it's something that's sensed. Their sense of our disapproval may cause them to be hesitant with us and not choose us to talk with about how bad it hurts to have lost a child.

Additionally our own disapproving nature, our own thought that they're not doing this very well may put distance between us and the grieving person. It may be difficult for us to help and comfort a person who is grieving in a way that seems so foreign and inappropriate to us. If we are aware of our own coping style and of how we grieve it is easier to set our expectations aside and be open to what the grieving person is telling us. Being conscious of making a judgment makes it possible not to make it.

We are not born knowing how to cope or grieve. Coping and grieving are things we learn, we are taught, and we develop on our own from the time we are infants in the crib playing with a rattle, flailing it about until it flies out of our hand and is lost. Some infants will begin to cry right away. Others will begin to feel about the bed, trying to find the rattle. Already we see the beginning of individual differences developing in how people react to loss.

By the time we reach the age of adults, we've all had a lot of experience with loss, starting with the rattle in our crib, on up through our baseball gloves, dolls, teddy bears, high school boyfriend or girlfriend, graduation from high school or college, moving away from friends, and grandparents dying. Each time we experience a loss, we react, we respond, we cope, we grieve, and in the process, we develop our own particular coping style. The first step toward being able to help grieving people is to become aware of our coping style, our grieving process so that we can set it in the back of our mind as we listen carefully to the grieving person.

12

GRIEF AS ENERGY

In order to help people who are grieving, it is important to understand what grief is and what people experience as they try to cope with the loss of a child. Grief is a form of energy. It's energy that gets thrust into us against our will when we learn that our child has died. It's as if upon learning that death has occurred, someone has taken a giant hypodermic needle and injected us with a huge dose of an active ingredient called grief. This grief begins to permeate our system and affects us physically and mentally.

The effects of this grief are felt as long as this energy is present. The process of grieving is the long process of eliminating grief energy from our minds and bodies.

LENGTH OF GRIEF

One of the first things to understand in helping a parent cope with the death of a child is how long the normal grieving process takes. On the average, it will take a parent one and a half to two and a half years to, in any sense, get over the death of a child. When I say, "get over," I don't mean forget. In fact, most bereaved parents say that there's a sense in which they never get over the loss of their child. They still love the child and they never forget the child. Years later, if they see a boy dressed in a jacket like their son wore, with a haircut like their son had, or hear a song on the radio that their daughter used to play on the piano, they may burst into tears unexpectedly. This is a normal response. Healthy people react this way.

After a long while they are able to laugh again, to love again, and to experience a full, happy, normal life. Their life will always be different, however, because of the agony and grief felt following the death of their child.

It is important to understand how long the normal grieving process takes so that we don't put intentional or unintentional pressure on grieving parents to recover sooner than it is realistic to expect that they can. The very length of the grieving process becomes a problem for people going through it, because most parents never dream it will take so long to get over the death of their child.

Our first experience with death is likely to be with a great grandparent or grandparent, an aunt or an uncle, somebody we miss and mourn; but someone whose death does not radically affect our routine day to day life after a couple of weeks. So most of us and most of our friends and relatives have the idea that grief shouldn't last more than a few weeks or a few months. Sure, when it's a child or a spouse, it's going to last a little longer, but most people would never dream that it would last as long as a year, let alone two or three years.

WHY GRIEF TAKES SO LONG

Part of the reason for the lengthy grief following the death of a child is that a child's death is so unexpected. It's out of order, unnatural. We expect that our grandparents and parents will die before we do, and the chances are 50-50 that our spouse, or our brothers or sisters will die before we do. But never in our wildest dreams do we expect that our child will die before we do. This just isn't the way the world is supposed to be, this isn't the way God set things up, this isn't the way the natural order is . . . children do not die before their parents.

Parents expect to look after their children, keep them safe, and raise them to be normal, healthy adults. When a child dies, it's as if the rug has been pulled out from underneath us. Something unnatural has occurred, the natural order of things has been disrupted. Not only do parents go through grief, they experience a threat and a challenge to their basic beliefs about the way the world is organized.

Their sense of security, their sense of trust in the universe or God is undermined. Without security, they feel threatened by a whole variety of things that would not have seemed threatening before their child's death.

A second reason that the parents' grieving process is usually so long and so difficult is that, just when they need help more than ever before, three of their major sources of strength and support in previous crises are likely to be denied them.

First, many friends and relatives will begin to stay away. They don't know what to say, they don't want to say the wrong thing, and they may be scared. A child has died and the grieving parent is a living reminder that their child could die too and that frightens them. They want to stay away from what frightens them. So because of their own fear or because they just don't know what to do and don't want to do the wrong thing, they may begin to avoid their friend whose child died.

Most bereaved parents say that their friendship patterns are realigned following the death of their child. Many people whom they considered their good friends stay away, and other people who had been no more than acquaintances come forward and become sources of support.

Second, the person least helpful to a bereaved parent in the grieving process is often his or her spouse. This causes tremendous difficulty in the grieving process. In a caring marriage, when her father died, or he had a bad day at work, the spouse was there to listen and to offer support. They tried to help one another as best they could. Now their child has died. Now they really need support, now they really need somebody to comfort them and as the wife is on her way to get support from her husband, he is on his way to get support from her. They discover they just don't have the strength to help each other.

Not only is each missing that source of support and that source of strength; but each begins to resent it, thinking "Where is he now when I really need him?" A gap is introduced into the marriage. Increasingly, the husband goes his own way, the wife goes her own way, and they are unable to help each other.

Furthermore, people grieve at different rates. A man is likely to grieve or react to loss in much the way his father did and a woman will likely react to loss or grieve much the way her mother did. It is unlikely that the husband and wife will grieve in the same way or at the same pace. The husband may be having a good day, just when his wife is having a bad day. His wife, having a bad day, not wanting to bring her husband down, may begin to avoid him, not say anything, and withdraw.

Sexual relations between husband and wife usually stop for a period following the death of a child, sometimes a prolonged period. This source of intimacy is also denied the grieving parent. The result of all this is that the marriage goes through a very difficult time following the loss of a child. Those of us wishing to be of help to a grieving person cannot count on the spouse as a source of support for bereaved parents. In rare instances husbands and wives will be able to support each other through the process, but more often they won't be able to and the marital relationship becomes part of the problem parents face as they grieve.

Finally, for those parents who are religious, have faith in God, and have been comforted by their faith before, the death of a child often undermines that faith. Some parents say that, without their religion and their faith in God, they would have never gotten through the grieving process. In my experience, such parents are a minority. A majority of parents, particularly if the child has died of a lingering illness, during which the parents and relatives have prayed for the child's recovery, react with a kind of anger at God, a disillusionment with God: "God is supposed to be all loving and all powerful, how could he have allowed this to happen to my child?" They begin to doubt. They begin to express anger. In any event, their faith and their belief in God are no longer available to help them through the grieving process.

Thus, right at a time when grieving parents need help the most, some of their friends will not be there, their husband or wife may not be able to support them, and their faith in God or religion may no longer be viewed as a source of support.

GRIEF AS A HEALING PROCESS

Going through a grieving process following the death of a child is actually a way of healing and recovering from a severe blow dealt to parents by their child's death. This psychological healing unfolds much as physical healing unfolds. For example, a person who receives a deep slash wound or breaks a bone goes into physical shock. This shock is a kind of protective device that keeps the enormity of the pain from hitting until the person can reach a clinic or doctor's office and get the wound cleaned out, stitched up, or the bone set. Grief works in much the same way.

When parents first learn that their child has died, they're likely to go into psychological shock. People who've experienced it describe it as "feeling numb; feeling like a zombie; feeling spaced-out like you're sort of in a fog. You hear what's said to you and yet you don't hear everything. Your mind is partially focused in present reality and partially not." This shock may last for weeks, it may last for months. It's a kind of protection that allows the enormity of what's happened to sink in gradually.

In physical healing, once the wound is stitched or the bone set, the injured person goes home. People are very attentive and solicitous, wanting to know what they can do for you or what they can get you. After a few days, however, they go back to their routine life and the injured person is left to cope with the injury as best he can. So it is with grief.

Around the time of the funeral and for the days and weeks that follow, newly bereaved parents may get a lot of attention. People will bring casseroles and call and the out of town relatives will come in to offer condolences; but before long, they go back to their routine life and the grieving parents are left with their child's toys, clothes, and vacant room. They are left to cope increasingly on their own.

A necessary part of physical healing involves opening the wound, taking the bandage off, letting it get a little air, cleaning it out, and then bandaging it up again for the healing to continue. It hurts to take the bandage off and disturb the wound, but it's a necessary part of the healing process. If the wound is kept tightly bandaged and the injured person pretends it's not there and hopes it will go away, it's only going to get infected, leading to a fever and other physical symptoms. If the healing is to take place the wound will have to be reopened and lanced, and the healing process allowed to start all over again.

Grief works in much the same way. Grief is one of those things you cannot go around, you cannot ignore; you have to go through the grieving process in order to heal. Nonetheless, we see many people who try to avoid grief, who hope it will go away, who deny it, trying to sweep it under the rug, pretending it isn't there and hoping to get on with their life as quickly as possible.

Men are more likely than women to try to avoid going through the grieving process. Many men have been taught since they were little boys that they have to be strong and tough and shouldn't cry. They carry this message with them into their adult life and react to some extent according to these rules when their child dies. Indeed many problems in therapy turn out to be related to unresolved grief.

For example, a 50-year-old man was able to recall the time when he was 10 years old, when his father died. A well-meaning aunt said to him at the funeral, "Now you've got to be strong for your mother, you're the oldest, you've got to be mother's little man now, she's going to really need you." The little boy, loving his mother, seeing her grief, and wanting to help her, did exactly that. He hid his grief and tried to be strong for his mother. That grief is still in him and will remain in him until he goes through a grieving process, in a year or two, or 40 years later.

Kahlil Gibran (1961) in his poetic essay on love describes what happens to people who are unable to grieve. "If in your fear, you would seek only love's peace and love's pleasure, then it is better that you cover your nakedness and pass out of love's threshing floor into that seasonless world where you laugh, but not all of your laughter and cry, but not all of your tears" (p. 12).

People who are unable to grieve, particularly men, often enter a seasonless world. They protect themselves from the pain of losing their child and, in the process, cut off the joy of living. They don't fully experience the ups or the downs of living. They're mildly depressed, they function, and live a fairly normal life, but something in them is missing, the ability to express or communicate deep feeling seems to be gone. With its absence a kind of distance grows between them and other people because they never allow anyone into their inner world, which is filled with the grief they were unable to express.

NATURAL HEALING PROCESS

The most important thing about grieving is to do it, to go through the process of healing. To let the natural healing process in you work by letting the feelings of sadness, anger, and guilt that are in you come out. There is within each of us a natural healing process that works. We see it most clearly with a physical wound, a deep slash wound, or a cut from peeling an apple. The wound will heal. It won't heal instantaneously, it may take a while, but it heals slowly, from within, and we get better.

Significantly, there is nothing that a physician can do or that anyone can do to make that wound heal any faster than it does. It can't be forced to heal. Grief works the same way. We can't force people through the grieving process quickly. They'll get better as they grieve, but it takes time.

Yet, most people who have contact with bereaved parents will, out of the best of intentions, put pressure on them to stop grieving, to get over it, to move through the process quickly. They care about the grieving parents and don't want to see the parents hurting, upset, or depressed. They want the parents to be over the pain. They say and do things designed to make the bereaved parent get better quickly.

It's our job as counselors not to pressure people to get better, not to hurry them through the grieving process, which is not possible anyway; but to be with them and allow this natural healing process to work.

DENIAL AS A PART OF GRIEVING

Before outlining what we as counselors can do to help bereaved parents through their grief, let me explain in a little more detail what the usual course of grief is like for most bereaved parents.

During and after the initial shock, which may last months, may come various kinds of denial. The simplest kind of denial is, in a sense, not denial at all, but a normal, subconscious process of not truly realizing the child is dead. In their minds, the parents know their child has died, but a part of them doesn't accept it. Indeed, for many parents, it is months before they're actually able to say, "My child is dead and I will not see him again on this earth."

This form of denial is illustrated by the mother who walks to the front window of her living room at 3:15 when the school bus used to let her daughter off. She stands there waiting before it suddenly dawns on her that her daughter won't be getting off the bus, her daughter's dead. Then she wonders, "What's the matter with me, how could I have forgotten my daughter is dead?"

The alarm goes off at 6:45 in the morning. The father gets up and walks down the hallway, puts his hand on the door to go in and wake his son for school before it suddenly hits him, "There's nobody in that bed. My son is dead," and again, he wonders how he could have forgotten that? He begins to wonder, "Am I losing my mind? What's the matter with me?"

There's nothing unusual about such experiences, yet sometimes grieving people may not know that they are normal and may feel disturbed and that their sanity is threatened.

Another kind of denial is learned as a way to cope with loss, pain, and grief. The most extreme form of this denial that I've encountered was a man whose teenage son was killed in a motorcycle accident. He came home from the funeral; went into his son's room; gathered all his trophies, posters, and clothes, boxed them up and got rid of them. He then took his son's photographs out of the photograph album, called his family together and said, "I do not want the name of our son ever mentioned again in this house." Of course this made life very difficult for his other children and his wife. His form of denial was so strong that it was not only a denial of death, but also a denial that life had ever existed.

With a person who needs to deny to that extent, it's important I think, for counselors to understand how much pain this man must be feeling that he needs to deny the very existence of his son. It's easy to blame such a person and to try to get him to face reality and to grieve. But usually trying to get somebody to do something that's not part of his way of coping is unlikely to be helpful.

This father had used extreme denial to cope with other losses and pains in his life. He didn't suddenly start denying when his son died. His father before him probably grieved or didn't grieve in the same way. With such people, the most likely form of help that we can offer is to accept their denial. Such people are not likely to seek counseling because they don't have a problem ("What son?"). To the extent that we encounter people denying like this, we do far better to accept them. Let them pretend it didn't happen, let them sweep it under the rug, and don't try to force them to deal with it.

Whenever we force somebody to try to deal with something they don't want to deal with, we bring out their defenses and we cause them to put energy into building up their defenses. We make their denial stronger. I think we do far better, even though there's no guarantee of success, to accept them with their denial. When they're with us they don't have to be defensive, they don't have to put energy into denying their son's life or death, they can relax, because we accept them as they are. The more we accept them, the less defensive they become. If there ever comes a time when they feel that they could risk talking a little bit about their child, they are more likely to do so with a counselor who makes them feel comfortable and safe and is not implicitly criticizing them, trying to get them to change, or trying to get them to deal with something they don't want to face. Accepting them as they are may be the most help we can offer a person using denial as a way of coping even though there is a good possibility that they may continue to deny their feelings indefinitely.

FEAR OF GOING CRAZY

For most grieving parents, grief is worse 6 to 12 months after the death than it is in the early weeks after their child died. This usually bewilders the grieving parent who thinks that after a few months, things ought to be getting better.

There are some very logical reasons why grief gets worse. The shock has worn off, the usual forms of denial begin to dissipate. Without thinking about it parents begin to cope with this child's death in whatever way they've learned to cope with previous losses.

After a few months, however, it is clear that these coping mechanisms are not working. They were not developed to cope with the death of a child. The death of a child is a whole new experience and many parents begin to think they cannot cope with it.

They fear losing control, losing their mind. In fact, it's extremely common for bereaved parents, 6 to 12 months following the death of their child, to enter a phase of grieving where they think they're going crazy. They'll come in for counseling and within five minutes they'll say, "You know, I just can't keep it together anymore. I think I'm losing my mind. I think I'm going crazy."

Part of the reason that grieving parents fear losing their mind is that, unfortunately, many of the symptoms of normal grief are also symptoms of mental illness: depression, paranoia, hallucinations. It's not uncommon to experience chronic clinical depression wherein they're depressed day after day. They have very little energy. It may be all they can do to get up in the morning. I know some bereaved mothers who didn't cook a meal for nearly a year following their child's death. They had hot dogs, TV dinners, or went out to MacDonald's, but cooking a family meal was more than they could manage. People who don't have to work will have days when they don't even get dresscd, but put on a housecoat, turn on the TV for company, and barely go through the motions of living. Whatever the symptoms, the inner depression is severe for many bereaved parents.

Hallucinations or visions in which parents think they see their dead child or think they hear their child calling from the next room sometimes occur. A mother whose 20-year-old daughter died of cancer was weeding flowers in front of her house when a car drove by. She happened to look up and see the driver who appeared to be a young woman about her daughter's age with a haircut like her daughter's. Glimpsed from the back the driver resembled her daughter. The mother couldn't help herself, she hurried to her car and followed the car of the young woman until it finally stopped. The driver got out and the mother could see that it was not her daughter. She felt foolish and silly. "What's the matter with me? I'm going crazy; of course that wasn't my daughter. My daughter's dead."

Some parents feel they've been singled out for some special kind of punishment. Some experience hallucinations, others are profoundly depressed, still others drink more than they're used to or take pills to prevent the painful thoughts from creeping into their minds. Occasionally, they become addicted to alcohol or to drugs and medication.

So many things combine to help parents reach the conclusion that maybe they're losing their minds. Added to them is the expectation that time should heal all wounds. They begin to think, "It's been 8 months, I should be getting better." Their friends think they should be getting better, saying "Don't you think it's about time that you were pulling out of this?" or "You seem to be really struggling. I wonder if you shouldn't seek professional help, see a psychiatrist, see a priest, whatever." The grieving parent begins to think "They're right, I am losing my mind, I should get professional help."

However, people grieving seldom need intensive therapy. They seldom need medication, which only submerges the grief and prevents the natural grieving process from unfolding. Grieving parents need some of the simplest forms of human interaction possible; they need someone to talk to, someone who will listen, someone who will understand and accept them as they struggle to cope with the death of their child.

WHAT COUNSELORS CAN DO TO HELP

There are three interrelated and equally important things that we counselors can do to help grieving people: (1) facilitate the release of their grief energy, (2) reassure them that their feelings are normal, and (3) put them in touch with other grieving people.

Release of Energy

Grief, this energy that's been thrust into bereaved parents against their will, has to be released. Anything that the grieving people can do to release it is going to facilitate the grieving process.

The first of the things to help release the grief is to talk, talk about their child who died, the day he or she died, what happened, what the doctor said, what was their first thought when the telephone call came, the good times they had with their child. In talking about the death, their feelings since the death, or the child who died, they are getting their energy out and facilitating healing. Those of us who would be helpful have to be good listeners. We have to provide the environment in which the grieving person feels comfortable, safe, and accepted as they share their feelings and thoughts.

A second way to release the grief is to cry. Crying is an ally in the grieving process. There's some evidence that tears shed in grief and sorrow are chemically different than other kinds of tears. Specifically, they contain more toxic substances so that when we cry, we're literally getting the poisons out, ridding our bodies of the things that are making us feel bad, cleansing our bodies, and making us feel better (Frey II, 1980). Crying is one of the most important ways of getting the sadness out.

When a person begins to cry, it's not so helpful to reassure them and say, "There, there now, don't cry. Everything's going to be O.K." Sometimes this shuts off the tears prematurely. It is often better to wait, listen, let the tears come, let the sadness flow, let the sobs pour out. After the energy has been spent it is time to hold them or comfort them, letting them know that we care for them and are concerned about them.

A third thing that helps get the grief out is the expression of anger. Most grieving parents feel anger when their child dies. They're often angry at God, the doctor, the other driver, their spouses, and sometimes even the child who died.

It is important that the grieving person acknowledge this anger, be helped to get in touch with it, and then express it. It's not necessary to express anger directly to the person toward whom it's felt. What's necessary is to think of the person we're angry with and think about what's making us angry, then to express that anger whether by pounding the table, beating the pillow, screaming in the car, or cursing while driving down the highway.

A car tends to be one of the few places where people can say whatever they want or scream whenever they want and nobody's going to hear them, they're not going to be embarrassed. Some parents I've talked with put a bucket over their heads and hollered into it. Others have written letters, even if never mailed, or kept a journal, pouring their angry feelings out onto the paper, which is a good way to express anger.

A fourth thing that's helpful is exercise. Exercise is especially helpful for people, often men, who have difficulty expressing emotions. Exercise is a good way of releasing energy. It is not so effective, however, unless the hurtful feelings (e.g. guilt, anger, sadness, etc.) are kept in mind during the exercise. A person's thoughts at the time the energy is released affect the benefits of releasing that energy. Hence to express anger when unaware of the source of anger, to cry when unaware of what's creating the sadness, to exercise when unaware of grief doesn't help as much as if, with his or her grief in mind, the parent jogs, runs up and down the stairs, swims, does push-ups, or walks.

The wife of a man whose daughter was murdered was very concerned about him because he didn't seem to be grieving. When conversation at the dinner table concerned his daughter he would look down or sometimes get up and walk away from his meal. In talking to the husband it turned out that every morning before work, he jogs. Nobody sees him and he says, "I'm not running more than 2 or 3 minutes before the tears start to come. I think about my daughter and I cry as I run. Sometimes my thoughts, my feelings turn to anger and I find that I'm running faster than I ever thought I could . . . I think about how angry I am about her being murdered and the person that murdered her. Then I go home, take a shower, cleanse myself, purge myself so to speak of my grief . . . the rest of the day, I don't want to think about it . . . I don't want to be reminded, I just want to get through the day. The next morning, I'm back out there running again." This is his way of grieving.

Creative work of some sort can be a good channel for grief. An artist or musician who can pour himself into work may find in creativity a good outlet for grief. Indeed any work often helps the grieving process. People who return to work usually cope with their child's death a little better than people who stay home with nothing to occupy their time and use up their energy. Any kind of work or creative activity will help, however.

A man whose child died of sudden infant death syndrome set about carving a wooden headstone for his son's grave. He didn't grieve openly and didn't talk to people about his grief. It took him almost 2 years to carve that headstone. When he finished, he took it to the cemetery and his grief seemed to be over. He seemed freed of the burden he had carried for 2 years. His energy had been channeled into this creative activity.

A final kind of energy that many parents need to express is their feelings of guilt. Because parents think they're supposed to protect their children and keep them safe from harm, they have a sense of failure when their child dies. They tend to feel guilty.

It is best to think of guilt as energy that needs to be released. The grieving parents should be encouraged to talk about their guilt, to talk about how bad it feels, how it's all their fault, how if only they had done this or hadn't done that everything would have been all right. One approach that I find helps is to encourage the guilt-stricken parent to see that their motives were good. In allowing his daughter to swim next door did the father intend for her to die? Of course not! In putting off her son's doctor's appointment did the mother intend for him to develop leukemia? Of course not! Parents are not guilty of their child's death.

In summary, the first thing we can do to help people grieve is to help them get their energy out. Talking, crying, expressing anger, expressing guilt, exercise, creative work, or anything else that helps get the energy out will help.

Reassurance

The second thing that helps grieving people is to let them know that they're not alone. Because so many bizarre behaviors and feelings come to grieving people in the grieving process, one of the most helpful things that a counselor can do after listening to grieving parents talk about their feelings is to let them know that their behaviors and thoughts are normal. Mentioning other people who have gone through similar things and giving examples helps parents to realize that they're not abnormal, they're not crazy, they're not losing their minds—but they are in grief. So many of the symptoms of grief happen to be symptoms of mental illness that reassurance that they're not crazy may comfort them as much as anything we can do.

Keeping the child's room intact for months after the death, which is a very normal response to a child's death, may upset friends or relatives who think the parents are making a shrine of the room. If the mother tells them that she's kept the room more or less the way it was when her child died and that every so often she goes in there in the evening, sits on the bed in the dark, thinks about her child, and cries a little bit; her friends and relatives think, "What's the matter with her? Why on earth does she go in there when she knows she's going to feel bad? Why doesn't she stop?'' This attitude indicates that they don't understand how long the grieving process takes and makes her feel that maybe she's doing something wrong, maybe she shouldn't be going in there, maybe she should clean out the room.

After her baby died, a young mother found some bibs that her child had thrown up on. She saved these bibs; every so often she took them out and smelled them, even though they smelled terrible, because the odor of her child was still on them. Another mother saved her 15-year-old son's dirty underwear for months after he died because the odor of her son was still on it. These are relatively normal behaviors for people in the grieving process, but people who know parents doing these things often think them strange and wonder if the parents need psychiatric help.

Few bereaved parents need psychological treatment for grief. They just need someone to be there with them, to listen to them, to accept them, and to allow them to move through the grieving process at their own rate.

Friends and relatives care about the parents whose child has died. It upsets them that the parents are still in grief and they want the grieving parents to get over it and be the way the used to be. So they say, "Don't you think it's about time that you got rid of Johnny's clothes?" "Don't you think it's about time you got out and started doing things?" "You can have other children." All of which shows that they want the grieving parent to stop grieving. Yet, normally bereaved parents won't be able to or, in a sense, even want to stop grieving during the first year or two following their child's death.

When I say, won't want to stop grieving, I mean that in order to stop grieving, parents have to let go of the child that died. They have to reach a point where they say, "My child is dead, but I am alive and I have the rest of my life to live. I'll never forget him, but I have to move on. I have to let go." Parents who have lost a child still love that child. They still have days when they cry about the loss, but they move on and live their lives in a fulfilling way; they let go.

It's not possible, in my experience, to let go during the first year or year and a half. It takes a long time. So if we wish to help grieving people, we have to understand that and not put pressure on them to finish their grieving before it's realistic for them to do so.

During this grieving process, one of the things that helps so much and takes some of the pressure off is to simply let the grieving parents know that what they're going through is normal. There's almost nothing that is abnormal during the first year of grief. To reassure parents that they're not crazy is one of the most helpful things we can do.

Support Groups

A third thing that helps is related to the first two; put grieving people in touch with other grieving people. It seems to be more potent to talk, cry, and express anger with other people, especially other people who understand because they're going through, or have recently been through a similar experience. Helping bereaved parents find each other so they can talk on the phone, have lunch together, go to support group meetings like Compassionate Friends[1] is a very constructive thing we counselors can do.

Another benefit that comes from interactions among grieving people is that newly bereaved parents can talk to bereaved parents who are further along in the grieving process. Those who are near the end of their grief and are doing fairly well provide inspiration to the newly bereaved, who may wonder if they'll ever be O.K. again, if they'll ever be able to laugh again, if they'll ever survive this tragedy.

In conclusion, we as counselors, in addition to encouraging parents to grieve, can reassure them that they're normal and not treat them as if they're crazy and can put them in touch with each other. Often, that may be the most helpful thing that we do: letting people with similar experiences help each other out as they go through the worst tragedy of their life.

------

[1]Compassionate Friends, P.O. Box 1347, Oak Brook, IL 60521.

REFERENCES

Frey II, W.H. Not-so-idle tears. *Psychology Today* 1980, *8*(13), 91–92.

Gibran, K. *The prophet.* New York: Knopf, 1961.

3. Helping the Partner of the Cancer Patient

Betty Satterwhite Stevenson
University of Rochester
Rochester, New York

ONCE THE DIAGNOSIS, CANCER, IS PRONOUNCED TO THE PERSON HE OR she loves, the life of the patient's partner* will never be the same. Although today about 45% of Americans in whom cancer is diagnosed will live 5 or more years, the word *cancer* is still equated with pain, disfigurement, debilitation, and death. Indeed, the strides of modern medicine have "changed cancer from an acute to a chronic catastrophe. The family system of a cancer patient moves therefore into a state of 'limbo' where interactions, plans, and socioeconomic realities are continually imbalanced and ever changing" (Cohen & Wellisch, 1978, p. 561).

PROBLEMS OF THE PARTNER

While dealing with the patient's (by now well-known) stages of grief described by Kubler-Ross (1969), the partner must pass through similar stages of grief. The partner must also cope with "feelings of anger at the prospect of being abandoned, guilt for the spontaneous feelings of anger, as well as his or her perceived omissions and failures in the relationship. Additionally he or she must work through. . . elements of 'survivor guilt,' . . . needs to justify his or her own continuing existence" (Ramshorn, 1974, pp. 247–248), in the event the patient dies. The errors in the relationship mentioned by Ramshorn were poignantly documented by Anderson (1974). The if I hads, if I hadn'ts, I should haves, I shouldn't haves endlessly plague the partner. Anderson added that "in times of strain such as this, one looks for support and, being human for comfort. The desperately needful man shocks the anguished husband. Absolutes come crashing down" (pp. 73–74).

It becomes the responsibility of the partner to attempt to maintain some degree of homeostasis in the family for the remainder of the patient's life. The partner must cope with the practical issues of family economics, especially if the patient is the primary breadwinner; what to tell their children, especially if they have not reached maturity; and what to tell the patient's parents, especially if they are elderly. In short, the partner must assume all the responsibilities formerly handled by the patient if the latter is too ill. The partner must also be the "buffer" between the patient and their children, their parents, other relatives, and their friends. All of these people are grieving too and may react in ways that exacerbate the stress being experienced by the partner.

---

*The word *partner* will be used in this article rather than husband, wife, spouse, or significant other in deference to nontraditional life styles.

There is a "paucity of information describing the psychosocial impact of cancer on adult family members of adult cancer patients" (Welch, 1982, p. 149). One thing is certain, however; the family therapist or counselor who accepts such a referral or consultation faces a complicated case. "The family must be assessed as to (1) its developmental level, (2) its unique style, and (3) patterns of interaction and their flexibility in times of stress" (Cohen & Wellisch, 1978, p. 563).

NEED FOR INFORMATION

If there is a dearth of descriptive information about the impact of cancer on the patient's partner, there is even less prescriptive information. The practical suggestions presented here for those who seek to help the partners of cancer patients come from the following sources: (1) my own life experiences, as my husband lived with bronchogenic carcinoma from 1964 to 1972 and my "avocation" since that time has been serving as a member of the National Board of Directors of the United Cancer Council and as a friend to many families who are "walking the same road," and (2) the experiences of volunteers in the Genesee Region Home Care Association Hospice Program in Rochester, New York, which is sponsored by the local United Cancer Council.

Partners seek help from a professional because they are finding it difficult to cope with the problems. They may have received insufficient information on the disease, or wrong information (or information they have misinterpreted), or conflicting information. In order to be helpful, the therapist/counselor must know the medical status of the patient. It is very possible that this will allow the professional to reassure the partner because of the higher survival rates seen today. It is unfortunate that survivors do not speak more loudly and clearly about their return to good health.

Patients and their partners may be very poorly informed regarding the actual medical condition. This is not to be critical of physicians. The pronouncement of a frightening diagnosis can be so devastating that oral explanations are often not perceived or understood. Studies have shown that families of children with spina bifida and juvenile arthritis, for example, lacked knowledge of the conditions, although physicians insisted they had explained it (Kanthor, Pless, Satterwhite, & Myers, 1974; Pless & Satterwhite, 1978). Family members need to be encouraged to write lists of questions for the physician and to request written information to be read when the content can be comprehended. Knowledge and coping have been shown to be positively correlated (Sahler, Satterwhite, & Reynolds, 1981). Of course, the professional must be aware that, for some, coping is dependent on denial.

It is also important for professionals to ensure that cancer information sought by patients and family members is current and medically accurate. Resource materials in public libraries, for example, may very well be obsolete. Incorrect information can be worse than no information.

EMOTIONAL NEEDS

Partners of cancer patients seek a therapist/counselor who will listen and with whom they can develop an honest, supportive relationship in which anything can be said. The professional must therefore be honest at all times. A lie ''quickly destroys any validity the therapist has and turns it (the relationship) into a mere discussion of permissable subjects between acquaintances'' (Le Shan, 1977, pp. 24–25).

There is a deep, unexpressed, almost universal fear among the partners of cancer patients that must be brought to the surface—the fear that cancer is contagious. Every partner of a cancer patient to whom I have mentioned this has said that he or she had thought about it. It is particularly true when the reproductive organs are involved. One patient recently told me amid tears that her husband had not touched her since her cancer had been diagnosed 5 years before! To the present, all studies show that cancer is not communicable. Although two studies have attempted to show an increased prevalence of cervical cancer in wives of penile cancer patients, no causal relationship has been proved (Graham, Priore, Graham, Browne, Burnett, & West, 1979; Smith, Kinlen, White, Adelstein, & Fox, 1980).

When a patient is coping with cancer, expressed love is more important than ever. Patients may feel that they are no longer desirable, however, while their partners may only be worried about somehow physically hurting them. Communication about this terribly important aspect of living is vital. To love and to be loved improves the coping capacity of all human beings.

Discussion of business matters should be encouraged. Wills, funeral arrangements, and the distribution of personal items are topics the patient and partner often avoid, although each may wish the other would initiate such a discussion. If these matters are not dealt with, they become difficult, often guilt-laden, problems for the survivor. Actually, dealing with these things is also beneficial to the patient, since it gives the patient control over something at a time when he or she feels powerless.

The partner may feel guilty when away from the patient. Respite for the partner should be encouraged, however. Physical weariness results from performing extra chores, caring for the patient, and not sleeping well. The partner should be encouraged to seek help through the hospital social worker or a comparable professional for home care assistance if it is needed.

HELPFUL RESOURCES

In coming to terms with cancer, partners need to be encouraged to reach out to friends who can listen and share, to express their fears and concerns, and to know that those fears and concerns are common to everyone who has been in the same situation. Because of the great mobility and isolation of families in the United States today, some of the support systems taken for granted in a previous generation are not in place. Extended family may live elsewhere; friends and neighbors may be in short supply. For these reasons, support organizations have sprung up to fill the gap, and they can be very helpful.

Make Today Count is a nonprofit support group for those with life-threatening illnesses, their families, and other interested persons. There are at present over 250 chapters in the United States and abroad. Cancer Hopefuls United for Mutual Support (CHUMS) is a new self-help group that gives men and women with a history of cancer the opportunity to meet one another for mutual support. The American Cancer Society, the United Cancer Council, and the Leukemia Society are among those organizations that have programs to help cancer patients and their families. The addresses of the national headquarters of these and other helpful organizations are

American Cancer Society
777 Third Avenue
New York, New York 10017

Concern for Dying
250 W. 57th Street
New York, New York 10019

Leukemia Society
800 Second Avenue
New York, New York 10017

Office of Cancer Communications
National Cancer Institute
Bethesda, Maryland 20205 (800-638-6694, a toll-free number)

United Cancer Council
1803 N. Meridian Street, Room 202
Indianapolis, Indiana 46202

Center for Independent Living
2539 Telegraph Avenue
Berkeley, California 94704

Cancer Hopefuls United for Mutual Support (CHUMS)
3310 Rochambeau Avenue
New York, New York 10467

Hodgkin's Disease and Lymphoma Organization
518 Wingate Drive
East Meadow, New York 11554

International Association of Laryngectomees
c/o American Cancer Society
777 Third Avenue
New York, New York 10017

Make Today Count
1803 N. Meridian Street
Indianapolis, Indiana 46202

National Amputation Foundation
12-45 150th Street
Whitestone, New York 11357

National Association of the Physically Handicapped
6473 Grandville
Detroit, Michigan 48228

National Self-Help Clearinghouse
184 Fifth Avenue
New York, New York 10010

Reach to Recovery
c/o American Cancer Society
777 Third Avenue
New York, New York 10017

Society for Rehabilitation of the Facially Disfigured
550 First Avenue
New York, New York 10016

United Ostomy Association
1111 Wilshire Boulevard
Los Angeles, California 90017

Their local chapters, along with hospital social workers, can suggest many other organizations designed to assist in patient care, e.g., Medical Motor Service and Meals on Wheels.

If the partners of cancer patients are at all religious, they may find help in their church. Their faith system, whether or not important before, can achieve new meaning. Suffering and death are viewed in different ways by different religions, but all have succor and love to give. The church can also provide a unique and caring support system through its community of believers.

CONCLUSION

If the cancer patient recovers or has time for living left, a warm and loving relationship with a partner can become enriched and even more beautiful. Values will change, and the important and certain things in life will be more cherished. Both patient and partner can grow and be better people, able to reach out and help others as they have been helped.

If the partner becomes the survivor of a loving relationship, the anticipatory grief already experienced can make the hard task of coping with loss easier. The experience of coping with cancer or any life-threatening illness of a partner is a "process that needs to be recognized for its naturalness, its productiveness, and its ability to bind us together in a common situation which reminds us of our universal selfhood" (Reed, 1974, p. 356). It is worth remembering that the survivor passes *through* the valley of the shadow of death. The survivor who has grieved well emerges whole and with a new commitment to make what has happened count toward a better tomorrow for others.

Postscript

Since agreeing to write this article, the author has become a cancer patient and would like to dedicate this article to her new and very loving husband, Mortimer E. Stevenson.

REFERENCES

Anderson, R. Notes from a survivor. In S. Troup & W. Green (Eds.), *The patient, death, and the family*. New York: Charles Scribner's Sons, 1975.

Cohen, M., & Wellisch, D. Living in limbo: Psychosocial intervention in families with a cancer patient. *American Journal of Psychotherapy* 1978, *32*(4), 561–563.

Graham, S., Priore, R., Graham, M., Browne, R., Burnett, W., & West, D. Genital cancer in wives of penile cancer patients. *Cancer* 1979, *44*, 1870–1874.

Kanthor, H., Pless, I., Satterwhite, B., & Myers, G. Areas of responsibility in the health care of multiply handicapped children. *Pediatrics* 1974, *54*, 779.

Kubler-Ross, E. *On death and dying*. New York: Macmillan, 1969.

Le Shan, L. *You can fight for your life*. New York: Jove/HBJ Book, 1977, pp. 24–25.

Pless, I., & Satterwhite, B. Division, duplication and neglect: Patterns of care for children with chronic physical disorders. *Child Care Health Development* 1978, *4*, 9.

Ramshorn, M. Selected tasks for the dying patient and family members. In B. Schoenberg, A. Carr, A. Kutsher, D. Peretz, & I. Goldberg (Eds.), *Anticipatory grief*. New York: Columbia University Press, 1974.

Reed, A. Anticipatory grief work. In B. Schoenberg et al. (Eds.), *Anticipatory grief*. New York: Columbia University Press, 1974.

Sahler, O., Satterwhite, B., & Reynolds, J. The pediatric family-patient health education library: The issue of access to information. *Pediatrics*, 1981, *68*, 374.

Smith, P., Kinlen, L., White, G., Adelstein, A., & Fox, A. Mortality of wives of men dying with cancer of the penis. *British Journal of Cancer*, 1980, *41*, 422–428.

Welch, D. Anticipatory grief reactions in family members of adult patients. *Issues in Mental Health Nursing*, 1982, *4*, 149.

HELPFUL PAMPHLETS

Office of Cancer Communications, National Cancer Institute, *Taking time—support for people with cancer and the people who care about them*. Bethesda, MD: U.S. Department of Health and Human Services.

Ogg, E. *When a family faces cancer*. Public Affairs Pamphlet, 381 Park Avenue South, New York, NY 10016.

Doyle, N. *The dying person and the family*. Public Affairs Pamphlet, 381 Park Avenue South, New York, NY 10016.

4. Families Coping with Suicide

Iris Bolton
The Link Counseling Center
Atlanta, Georgia

SUICIDE INVOLVES MUCH MORE THAN THE DESTRUCTION OF THE PERSON who swallows an overdose of pills or pulls a trigger. Very often, it destroys others in the same family, burdening them with an indelible stigma and rupturing the bonds of interpersonal relationships that have endured for years. The real victim, time after time, is not the cold body in the coffin, but the family.

In Clearwater, Florida, Ken and Mary Whitney both worked, and their combined salaries were putting their three sons through college. Jock, the eldest, came home from the state university during spring break, climbed an oak tree, slipped a noose about his neck, and jumped. When Ken and Mary came home after work, they found his body twisting in the wind. No cause for suicide was apparent. Their shock was succeeded by guilt and then by anger. Mary accused Ken of being too hard on the boy for slight infractions. Ken charged Mary with coddling the boy and undermining a disciplinary program. The two surviving sons took sides, one for the father, one for the mother. A separation followed, then a bitterly fought divorce. Within months, that family was destroyed.

In Los Angeles, California, Joan and Tom Miller were planning to celebrate their 20th wedding anniversary with their son and daughter. Tom supported the family by traveling for a large corporation. Barbara, 15, came home unusually late that afternoon, smelled gas fumes coming from the garage, and found her mother's lifeless body sprawled over the steering wheel of her station wagon. No suicide note had been left, and there seemed to be no motive. The stunned family responded with disbelief and guilt. The father's drinking problem exploded into alcoholism. The daughter believed she could have saved her mother had she returned home on time. Her guilt was exaggerated because the ignition key had been switched off as if her mother had wanted to live at the last moment. The daughter's self-blame was further magnified because of a violent argument she had had with her mother the night before. The 12-year-old son, Jim, felt rejected and deserted by his mother. His fury was acted out during the following months by stealing a bike from a neighbor, destroying school property, and getting expelled from school. He was confined in juvenile detention as a ward of the state and is currently living in a foster home. The daughter, Barbara, despairing and guilt-ridden, attempted suicide herself and is now in a state treatment center for depressed adolescents. The father was fired from his job for refusal to enter an employee assistance program for alcoholics. Within the year, the family was destroyed.

Shneidman (1980) explained that certain kinds of death, such as murder and suicide, involve four powerful components that impose a particularly heavy burden: (1) the "stigma of murder or suicide," (2) "the specter that you yourself might suffer a similar fate," (3) thoughts by day and dreams by night that are filled with "disturbing images of blood and violence," and (4) "the obsession of the survivor with the whos, the whys, the whats, and the ifs." Such obsessions and such images clearly can become the wellsprings of disaster. Fortunately, disaster and disintegration of a surviving family are not inevitable.

POSTVENTION

This destructive burden can be obliterated and eliminated through the use of therapies and procedures that have been developed in recent years. Shneidman (1981, p. 349) has given this after suicide care the name of "postvention." It consists of "activities that serve to reduce the aftereffects of a traumatic event in the lives of survivors. Its purpose is to help survivors live longer, more productively, and less stressfully than they are likely to do otherwise" (p. 350). To that end, he developed a set of common sense principles (p. 358):

1. A counselor should begin working with "survivor victims" as soon as possible.
2. Most survivors eagerly welcome opportunities to talk to a professional.
3. Powerful negative emotions, such as irritation, anger, envy, shame, and guilt, should be expected. All these emotions must be explored and ventilated eventually.
4. The postvener plays the role of "reality tester." The counselor is "not the echo of conscience," but rather "the quiet voice of reason."
5. A medical examination by a physician is useful. Shneidman even called it crucial. These scientific findings can provide a base line for estimating improvement or deterioration of a client's physical or mental status.
6. All conversational banalities and Pollyannaish platitudes must be avoided.
7. The process of recovery from the traumatic loss of a loved one is often long, slow, and punctuated by setbacks. Shneidman said that postven-

tion takes a full 3 months at least and may take a year. Occasionally, it is needed to the end of life.

8. "A comprehensive program of health care . . . should include preventive, interventive and postventive elements" (Shneidman, 1980, p. 358).

To Shneidman's list of basic principles, the following basic fears, as voiced by several mourners soon after a suicide in their family, could be added:

- "Since my loved one preferred death to life with me, I must be at fault . . . I must be a 'bad' person. I must have caused the suicide."
- "I'm going crazy."
- "Nobody else feels the intensity of pain and anguish as I do, thus, nobody else can understand my despair . . . my agony."
- "I won't be able to live without this person."
- "Perhaps suicide is inherited . . . maybe another member of my family will commit suicide . . . maybe even me."
- "I really don't want to live either, but I can't admit that. I don't think I can go on living . . . there is no hope for me."
- "What will my friends think of me . . . of our family? Everyone will think I am a bad person . . . that we are a bad family. How can I ever face anyone again?"
- "My husband was in such trouble emotionally, I even felt relief when I heard he was dead. I feel guilty about that, too."
- "I'll never stop reliving the moment I discovered her."
- "If I really let go, I'd be out of control and I'd explode."
- "Professionals can't help or understand if they haven't lost a loved one to suicide. No one can help me."

INDIVIDUAL AND FAMILY DYNAMICS

The mourning process takes place in three areas almost simultaneously—within the individual, within the family, and within the social environment (i.e., the community). The three areas are interrelated and weave a web of protection or destruction, depending on many complex factors.

Each family member uniquely responds to a suicide, as does each family group and each community. The father of a 15-year-old boy who shot himself to death 6 months ago stated, "You make your own grieving process. It's neither right or wrong . . . it just is!" The response depends on the individual, the dynamics and structure of the family, and, to some degree, on the attitudes of the community. Although the response and the needs are different in each situation, the therapist may find it helpful to examine a number of variables that may affect the healing of the individual survivor and, ultimately, the healing of the family:

1. basic self-esteem or feelings of worth. If the client's self-esteem is low, the therapist can expect more difficulty with recovery, especially around the issue of guilt.
2. the ability and willingness to express feelings to others. Denying or hiding feelings may lead to isolation and depression.
3. relationship to the deceased. Who died? Was it mother, father, child, spouse? Was the relationship positive or negative?
4. knowledge of the grief process and history of handling loss. What does the client know about the grief process? Does the client need to be told what to expect? Do past experiences in dealing with loss or death give the client a sense of hope that he or she will survive this loss?
5. acceptance of humanness of self. Is the client aware that life encompasses both success and failure? This may determine how guilt is resolved and whether it can be turned into regret through forgiveness of self and others.
6. experience with handling stress and solving problems. Strength, courage, and hope may be gained from past experiences.
7. age of the mourner. During certain stages of development, the impact of suicide may be more severe, such as during adolescence.
8. the support system. Is the client isolated, or are there friends/peers available for sharing and support?
9. spirituality or religious resources and beliefs. What are the client's attitudes toward God, death, suicide, the meaning of life, and afterlife?
10. attitude toward professional help.

The therapist can sense many of these aspects of the individual client's personality and may also choose to ask direct questions.

Not only do these 10 components serve as a guide in the journey of healing for individual clients, but also they provide important information regarding the dynamics of the family's grief process.

1. How does the family generally feel about themselves *as a family?*
2. How does the family communicate within their group? Is it an open or closed system?
3. Who died in the family, and what was that person's role? What difference will that person's absence make in the family constellation? How will the family be reorganized?
4. What does this family know about grief? What do they need to know? What is the family history of handling loss? Have they faced other deaths as a family or shared other losses?
5. Do family members accept each other as human beings who sometimes succeed and sometimes fail, thus paving the way for dealing with guilt?
6. What is the family experience in dealing with stress and in solving problems together as a family?
7. What are the ages of all family members? Is anyone going through a difficult life stage, such as adolescence or retirement?
8. What is the family's support system? Is there a close group of neighbors, friends, or church community?
9. What is the family consciousness regarding spirituality, religious traditions, attitudes and beliefs about death, life, and afterlife?
10. Is the family open to seeking outside help if necessary, or are they determined to "go it alone" no matter what?

Shneidman's basic tenets of postvention, the common fears of suicide survivors, and the dynamics of individuals and families provide a bare framework on which the therapist and the family weave their tapestry of grief work and healing.

PERSONAL EXPERIENCE

These concepts have served me well in understanding my own role as a suicide survivor and, subsequently, as a grief counselor following the traumatic suicide of my own 20-year-old son in 1977. What happened to me was typically blinding, maddening, and paralyzing.

On a Saturday morning in February, my second-born son, Mitch, shot himself in his bed with two guns while talking to his ex-girlfriend on the telephone. He was a bright, popular, attractive young man whose sadness prior to his death had seemed to be related to his girlfriend's rejection of him. We now believe his depression was masked and that it covered a deep despair and overwhelming pain so paralyzing and debilitating that he chose to die rather than live with it.

As the first days passed, not a single ray of hope penetrated the blackness that gripped my mind. Literally, I can still remember the exact words that introduced me to postvention therapy and made my recovery possible. "You will survive," the man said. His gaze locked my eyes to his. I sensed his sincerity and his determination that I should share his vision. The man was Dr. Leonard T. Maholick, an Atlanta psychiatrist and an old friend. "You will survive," he repeated firmly, "if you choose to." I wanted desperately to believe him. It was a beginning.

During the weeks and months that followed, my husband and I and our three remaining sons were to experience the healing balm of many services and experiences. We talked about how we could blame and destroy one another or we could survive together. Our decision, as a family, was to survive this crisis together, facing the truth and reality of the horror of suicide. We would deal with the stigma in the community, and we would not cover up the ugliness of this kind of death. We made funeral decisions in family conferences, seeking comfort and understanding from one another. We talked and shared and clung to each other; somehow, our collective pain was eased.

The presence of relatives arriving from all over the country, who held us, fed us, encouraged us, and loved us in spite of the stigmatizing tragedy that had befallen us, was the burgeoning womb from which our healing was to grow. The throngs of friends and acquaintances with outstretched arms who listened and kept a steady vigil throughout the endless blurring of days and nights added curative powers. Weekly therapy sessions allowed regular venting and purging of emotions, served as a guide for survival, and provided a sense of hope that we would survive.

A minister of a local Atlanta church, the Reverend Al Widener, asked me to join him in co-leading a group of bereaved parents from different faiths in a self-help group. His trust and faith in me as a "wounded healer" gave me a much needed boost by allowing me to become useful to myself and others, as well as to begin making meaning out of meaninglessness. After a year, the group joined a national organization called The Compassionate Friends, a support group for bereaved parents. It was in this group of struggling, grieving, healing parents that much grief work was done.

Another part of postvention was the encouragement to express our feelings, without judgment—negative or positive—to ourselves, to God, to the air, or to one another. We gave ourselves permission to cry, to talk, to feel, to write, to scream . . . to do whatever helped. This was necessary, and we were assured that we were not going crazy. It was a normal part of the grief process.

Not many weeks had passed before I found that my pain was soothed somehow by talking about it. I felt compelled to tell the story of our tragedy. When I hurt the most, my reaction was to talk about my son's death to whatever person was handy. Among others, I talked to my grocer, my pharmacist, and the man at the cleaners. Invariably, I felt better afterward. My husband's needs were different, as is often true with spouses. He was more private in his grief, and telling the story was not helpful to him. Both needs and differences are to be honored. Today, I ask my clients to share with others the details of their own experience as often as possible, if it helps them. For some, during the early weeks of their purgatory, it seems to cleanse and cool their spirits. Malcolm in Shakespeare's *Macbeth* says, "Give sorrow words: the grief that does not speak whispers the o'erfraught heart and bids it break. . ." (Act IV, Scene 3, line 209).

Another important discovery was that grief is a process of ups and downs. I had never known this. Initially, my own Humpty Dumpty reactions baffled me; one day I would be euphorically optimistic—I would survive—but the next would find me wrapped in the blackest fog. Learning about Kubler-Ross' grief research showing that all feelings were normal and that moods changed drastically and inevitably gave me a more powerful sedative than any drug. Now, for the first time, I had a road map. It was like discovering that I was driving through a mountain range where snowy mountain tops alternated with sunny valleys, but I was on a safe highway.

Another kind of mood during those early weeks also became a horrid puzzle. When it came, it came gradually. Its effect was that for a time I was calm and even peaceful. There was a sense of relief that my son was no longer suffering. Simultaneously, I was deeply ashamed of myself. To think that I could be relieved or at peace for an instant was obscene. No good mother could harbor such feelings. Terror hit me like a paralytic stroke. Maybe I was losing my mind. Was I? Had it happened to others? I had to know. Through postvention therapy, I learned that it was normal for me to feel a sense of peace or relief at times that my son's pain had ended when he pulled that trigger. An expert had written, I forget where, "A sense of relief when a difficult situation ends is normal." That line, I think, prevented my healthy feeling of relief from turning to poisonous guilt.

Soon after the initial shock faded, I remember that my mind spun endlessly in a quest for an answer to *why*. As a family, we had needed to know *how* it had happened; now we needed to know *why*. Although we searched our memories thoroughly, although we talked to friends and to scholars, we could reach no conclusion. Today, I have clients who perform the same ritual. At first, a childlike faith in logic drives them back along the highways of their lives. At what crossroads did they take a wrong turn? With what spoken word, what angry retort, did the disaster begin? I recall thinking that enough answers would allow me to wrap the mystery of suicide in a neat package and hide it forever on a closet shelf.

Many survivors are tempted to follow the example of their departed spouse, child, or friend. I spent many hours walking the razor's edge between life and suicide; but, reluctantly, I learned that I had options that are both nobler and more effective. For many persons, the desire to join the dead loved one is part of the process of grief.

Finally, I personally learned that a survivor is like a castaway marooned on an island surrounded by a river of floodwaters. Survivors are cut off, as I was cut off, from all human contact because they withdraw emotionally from others. Rising waters (recurrent agony) gradually reduce the chance of rescue. As the far shore recedes, voices fade and familiar faces vanish. I remember days when I lost all hope of rescue. Postvention therapy, skillfully administered, gradually turned my thoughts to self-rescue. I had been a strong swimmer. I still possessed skills and enjoyed robust strength. Might they ensure my salvation? A large mental effort, followed by a small physical effort, was what I needed. The latter was a telephone call to a friend who (in my mind) had deserted me. "I want to see you," I said. She replied, "I'll meet you in the park." We met and talked for hours. I called another friend. We also met. I called another . . .

Another truth about surviving suicide, as I discovered, is that many friends want to help, but do not know how. Longing to offer some comfort, they cannot find the words. When I reached out to them, however, they came to me with joy, and my flooded river was bridged by a dozen causeways.

THERAPEUTIC IMPERATIVES

Postvention is truly a multifaceted miracle. Although it remains a grossly neglected aspect of family therapy, those who practice it diligently are turning it into an effective instrument for healing. To summarize my own experience and that of my family, and to add to Shneidman's principles, I suggest these few imperatives:

1. Assure the family that they will survive.
2. Encourage the family to talk openly whenever possible about the experience, the pain, and the bafflement.
3. Teach the process of recovery from grief. It can be described as slowly ascending from basement to attic, climbing a series of stairsteps, one at a time, and occasionally stumbling and falling back.
4. When survivors insist that they want to die, let them know this is normal and will pass.
5. Teach survivors to reach out to other family members and to old friends. Friends and family can be the survivor's parachute. The fewer they are, the smaller the chute, the faster the fall. Reaching out ensures survival.
6. Finally, remember that a wound always leaves a scar. Clients say, "I can never forget what happened." Of course not. Time helps healing, however. One day they will remember the life of their loved one, not the death. Their life will never be the same again, nor will they ever be exactly the same people; but they must decide individually whether to live the remainder of their lives as angry, hostile people or as caring, compassionate people.

Bridges recently summarized his work with families in the aftermath of suicide as follows:

> First, encourage them to know it's all right to sit down and remember their life with this person. My belief is that in therapy they sit down and remember and that will enact the healing process and the grief process which has been tragically disengaged by the person's choosing to take life into his own hands. In that way the family member or members who have come for counseling are helping to bring order into their lives and in a mystical way bring order out of the chaos from which the suicide erupted.
>
> So, the sitting down is the beginning.
>
> Second is the remembering . . . and with the remembering, the acceptance begins to set in and after a while, the people are ready to adjust and get up and move on.

In assisting family survival in the aftermath of suicide, Hogan (1983) stressed the importance of "commitment to the survival of the family," as well as "commitment to the memory of the deceased." These two aspects are essential for positive resolution. Whether it is a child, a parent, a spouse, or a sibling who has committed suicide, the family system will be "in a crisis state as all of the pieces that fit together to make it a special family become disorganized and are then reorganized into a new, smaller family" (p. 1) She added that family members need to be assured that such disorganization normally occurs after a tragedy and that in time the family will have understandable rhythms again" (p. 1). As one bereaved father put it, "You never get over it, but it does get better." Families need to know that they will survive. *How* they survive is their choice. Some families blame each other and separate, while others pull together and become a stronger, more bonded group. The choice may depend on the overt hope for survival and the commitment to remember the deceased. In my own family, decisions were made as a group following my son's suicide. We had a consensus on the beliefs that we would survive together, that we would always remember his life, that we would never fully understand why suicide had occurred in our family, and that we did not need to know in order to go on with our lives. We did not understand it; we did not have to. We did not like it; we did not have to. We chose to survive as a family and as individuals in that family. We would value life and each other in a way not possible before.

BEREAVEMENT PROCESS

Research has contributed much to the understanding of the bereavement process, and many categories, phases, and stages have been offered. Parkes distinguished four phases: "numbness, yearning/protest, disorganization, and reorganization" (Schneidman, 1981, p. 352). Stone (1972) listed seven dynamics of grief: "shock, catharsis, depression, guilt, preoccupation with the loss, anger, and reality. The seven dynamics are to be considered as seven major aspects of an individual's typical pattern of adaption to the traumatic loss involved in death" (p. 27). He further stated that they are not a linear progression of stages; rather, they describe the seven major emotional dynamics which the bereaved experience, listed in the order they generally appear.

Stone further concluded that the major differences between the suicide and the nonsuicide grief occur in three areas. In the phase of catharsis, feelings about the suicide (the type of death) must be expressed. As the stigma and blame from others are perceived, the survivor often feels anger, shame, and guilt. During the period of depression, there is often more suicide ideation (i.e., "more self-destructive impulses and behavior among suicide survivors''), and they may "hold the grief within themselves more and act it out psychosomatically" (p. 45). Perhaps the major difference Stone observed is "the greater amount of guilt associated with the suicide death. Connected with this guilt is a greater amount of anger at the deceased" (p. 45).

CONCLUSION

Suicide is now occurring in the United States approximately 35,000 times each year. Some studies assert that a higher number—at least 100,000 annually—is more accurate. With every such death, probably at least four persons are catapulted into chaos. Without any preparation, they must deal with the loss of a family member. Invariably, they are stunned, dismayed, and disoriented. The violence of a self-inflicted death challenges their own assumption that modern life is worth living. Their lack of preparation, plus the violence of the act itself, guarantees their devastation. Their inability to determine the reason is mind-boggling. Society's cultural and religious bias against those touched by a suicidal death results in a stigma that further deepens wounds to body, mind, and spirit.

All these factors compose the suicide syndrome. It spreads to others beyond the family of origin. Grandparents, relatives, teachers, ministers, acquaintances, and neighbors hear of the event as its shock waves spread in all directions. Like the plagues of Europe's Middle Ages, suicide is feared by everyone and understood by no one. As yet, science has not isolated either a virus or an emotional distemper, but the walking wounded can be counted by the hundreds of thousands.

Until now, most therapists have been unprepared to assist in healing the bereaved, not that they have been complacent. Indeed, sociologists, psychologists, and psychiatrists have united in a gigantic effort to stem the rising suicide rate. The media, always hypnotized by the drama of multiple deaths, have encouraged the notion that a quick fix can somehow transform despondence into mental health. Suicidologists have even formalized a defensive formula that consists of prevention, intervention, and postvention. Yet, the world's ageless yearning for self-extinction continues—part escapism, part revenge, part pain killer, and part fad. Neither societal nostrums, psychological theories, nor chemotherapy works.

Like the poor, suicide survivors are still with us. Their number increases daily, and their need is great. It seems to me that their best hope—perhaps their only hope—lies in postvention.

REFERENCES

Bridges, J.E. Personal Communication, 1983.

Hogan, N. Commitment to survival (Part 2). *Compassionate Friends Newsletter*, 1983, 6(4), p. 1.

Kubler-Ross, E. On death and dying. New York: Macmillan, 1969.

Shneidman, E.S. *Voices of death*. New York: Harper & Row, 1980.

Shneidman, E.S. Postvention: The care of the bereaved. *Suicide and Life-Threatening Behavior, Suicide Thoughts and Reflections, 1960-1980,* 1981, 2(4), 358.

Stone, H.W. *Suicide and grief.* Philadelphia: Fortress Press, 1972.

5. Helping Children Cope with Death

Sandra Bertman
University of Massachusetts Medical School
Worcester, Massachusetts

WITH ALL THE QUIET MATURITY OF ADULTHOOD, WOODY ALLEN asserts that he is not afraid of death—he just doesn't want to be there when it happens. For adults as well as for children, death is an event associated with awe, with fearsome thoughts and emotions one would rather not entertain. Describing death as a highly desirable state, devoutly to be wished for, as God's will, or as a reward for good behavior might be an inspiration or a consolation for the Hamlets and saints of the world; it might well sow the seeds of wrongdoing or even of atheism for others. Indeed, Jesus Christ, facing his own death, cries out during those final moments, "Oh, Father, why hast thou forsaken me?"

Not only one's own dissolution, but any death, however distant or natural, gives rise to unsettling questions of personal vulnerability and mortality. In his poem, "Spring and Fall to a Young Child," Hopkins (1967) suggested that it is not the demise of a human being, but rather a "goldengrove unleaving," a change of seasons, that is cause for sobering grief. In the poem's concluding couplet, it is quite clear that the young girl, Margaret, has made the association between the death of any living thing and herself. No longer the childhood innocent, she has become aware of for whom it is the bell tolls:

> It is the blight man was born for,
> It is Margaret you mourn for.

On second glance, then, it is not only his own death that Woody Allen would choose not to attend; he would not want to be present at the death of anyone (or anything) else. If avoidance behavior is childlike, Woody Allen speaks for the child in all of us.

The attempt to protect oneself from the anguish of separation and the pain of bereavement is understandable, but it is inevitably unsuccessful. Grief *is* work. Most often described as a sequential process occurring in distinct stages (denial, depression, acceptance), grief requires close attendance (Bowlby, 1966). The only way to complete the mourning process (i.e., to work through the initial numbness and protest of denial, to detach hope and associations from the dead) is to experience it. A conscious acknowledgment of the disorganization, depression, fear, sadness, and anger is required before tranquil resolution is possible.

Much has been written about the stages of youngsters' understanding of death. In general, children under 5 years old view death as a reversible state, similar to life. These children have no concept of universality of psychological separation; they believe that the dead still breathe, sneeze, sleep, and play as they did in life or that, if not doing so now, they shall resume doing so wherever they are or whenever they come back. Children who are 5 to 9 years old personify death. Darth Vader-like, the deathman ("bogey man," skeleton, devil) takes one because of a whim or because of the child's bad behavior. Ultimately, when they are older than 9, youngsters come to the realization that death is a definitive state, inevitable, irreversible, and universal (Anthony, 1940; Nagy, 1959).

Such guidelines are useful, but clearly neither all-inclusive nor cast in concrete. The following story from a youngster cuts across at least two developmental levels and introduces other characteristics commonly expressed in elementary school classrooms in the 1970s and 1980s:

> Once upon a time a ball came floating down from outer space. The next morning, a boy went outside into the fields to play. He saw a big white ball. There was a red button on the white ball. He pushed the button. It started shaking and then it opened. A thing came out of it and the boy ran. It destroyed everything in sight, including the boy. A cop found it and called the dead boy's mother. Finally, they shot at it. And when they killed it, the boy came back to life.

Death is not only externally caused (by "the thing"), but also is violent and catastrophic ("It destroyed everything in sight, including the boy."). The entire description is objective; its focus is reminiscent of Solomon Grundy or Elinor Rigby (once born, once married, once dead). Although omnipotence is ascribed to the adults, no affect is given in connection with the boy, the cop, or the boy's mother. Only the neutral outline and the facts are provided. The boy's pushing the button might be considered an implication of his responsibility; unlike Pandora, however, the boy was not told to stifle his curiosity or refrain from opening or touching the object.

Youngsters do struggle with the concept of a just dessert. In German fairy tales, the misbehaviors of Augustus, who would not eat his soup, and Harriet, who disobeyed and played with matches, result in "appropriate" deaths; Augustus starved by wasting away, and Harriet was burned up by fire (Hoffman, 1944). American children are brought up with Pinocchio, whose deformity grows as his integrity slips. One youngster elevated misbehavior to the level of sinfulness. On the back of a paper towel, he wrote, pleading anxiously to a harsh, exacting God, "Oh, please, God, please, I don't want to die. Please. I will stop teasing and temper. Oh, God, please!" It is a mature adult, however, who freezes at the news of her husband's accidental death, harboring the belief that the event is fit punishment for her little tricks. In Kudret's "Feast of the Dead," Gulnaz rationalizes in a clearly unsuccessful attempt to convince herself: "No, oh no, God could not be that cruel. This could not be anything but an accident. There were witnesses: he slipped, fell down, and died. Anybody could fall this way and die" (1976, p. 162).

It appears that an individual's personal experiences with death, in conjunction with developmental level, are the barometer for that person's subsequent concepts of and attitudes toward death.

Patricia Hovey, an oncology social worker, reported a touching story of a 7-year-old coping with his mother's death. The day his mother died, the child walked out to his grandmother, who was hanging clothes in the backyard. "We're going to have to tell people Sally doesn't live here anymore." His hands held cards and letters addressed to his mom. "How do you spell died?" When his grandmother finished hanging the wash and went into the house, she found three signs Scotch-taped to the front and back doors and to the mailbox: "Sally Died Today."

Verbalization is one way of helping a child confront and accept a death. In a just-the-facts scenario about a young boy, Sam, whose grandmother dies, youngsters added the following revealing embellishments:

His grandmother was in the hospital and Sam could not see her because. . .
"He would catch her germs."
"She looked scary."
"She would cry."
"Sam would cry and cry, and his mother would be angry."
"Sam would be sad."
"She might die."

In the sequel scenario of having to tell a cousin or a younger sibling that Sam's grandmother has died, the youngsters are quick to unravel the tangles in the well-intended explanations. Saying "She went on a long trip." may cause problems the next time parents take a vacation or trip; saying "She went to sleep." may well result in insomnia; and saying "She died because she was sick." may cause a child to fear that the outcome will be death the next time someone gets sick. Religious explanations always generate interest and discussion. Sharing beliefs is a fine way to diffuse some of the amorphous terror that surrounds death and to develop a tolerance for different points of view and for ambiguity.

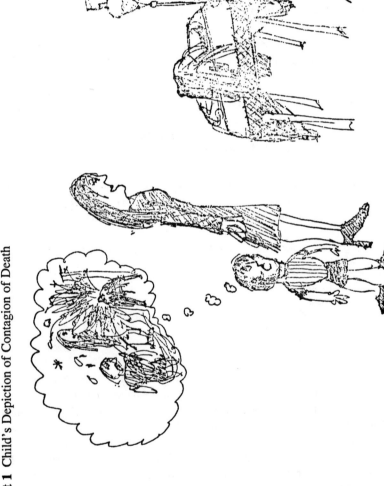

Exhibit 1 Child's Depiction of Contagion of Death

Drawings, play, and role plays in prescribed dramatic scenarios are wonderful ways to approach the concerns, fears, fantasies, and misconceptions of youngsters. By showing that they are not frightened of the subject or of the children's responses, therapists are often able to clear up misconceptions, allay anxieties, and provide reassurance that these responses are normal and acceptable. As is clear in Exhibit 1, the contagion aspect of witnessing a death is the issue for some youngsters.

PRIOR TO A SIGNIFICANT DEATH

Open communication with a child is warranted prior to a death in the family. The therapist should seek answers to the following questions. What are the sources of support for the youngster within the family? From the child, as well as from the family member, is it possible to assess whether the impending death has been discussed and with whom? Did the child or the parent initiate the conversation? How detailed was the discussion? Is the illness known to be cancer? Was the possibility of death mentioned?

Ideally, the concerns and unfinished business that might plague the youngster (and adults) in the future are elicited before the death occurs. Such questions as the following are appropriate for assessing the levels of knowledge and open communication in a family, as well as for facilitating anticipatory mourning:

- Can you tell me about your grandmother's illness? How serious is it? Might she die from it?
- Tell me about your grandmother. Did you two trim the Christmas tree together? Was she the one who taught you to sew? I'll bet there were some rough times the two of you had . . . what were some of the worst?
- Since Grandma became sick, what have you been feeling?
- How has her illness changed your life at home? At school?

In one episode of the TV series, *The Waltons,* young Jason does not want to accept a present from Seth, a friend of his who is dying. In group discussions, this behavior is interpreted as anger at the friend for putting him in such a discomforting situation or as magical thinking that, if he does not acknowledge the gift, perhaps his friend will not die. Grandpa Walton initiates a conversation about death and Jason's refusal to accept Seth's gift. He urges Jason to give way to his grief for his friend and for himself both in his heart and to his friend's face. The gift and the grief are symbolic of caring. Grandpa Walton penetrated the denial and facilitated mourning for his grandson by helping him to accept the reality of the situation.

The saying of goodbyes is to be encouraged. The child should be carefully prepared for a visit to a dying family member. What has happened, how the dying person might look or behave, and reasons for making the visit should be discussed. The child may want to bring a gift, a note, or a drawing to the ill or dying relative. Like Grandpa Walton, the therapist facilitates mourning by helping family members accept the reality of the situation and tend to their own emotional healing. Such direct confrontation does more than acknowledge the seriousness of the situation; it allays the paralysis of frustration and helplessness. Being able to grieve openly, especially in the midst of a loving family, is therapeutic for both the person dying and for the survivors. By accepting Seth's gift, Jason grieved both for himself and for his friend. Expression of how much the dying person matters and will be missed can be uplifting to everyone involved, as shown by the youngster's drawing in Exhibit 2. A young boy's cancer clearly changed his relationship with his brother for the better. As the young artist added, "They, both, will always know that."

AFTER THE DEATH

No matter how prepared the family is for the death, the event itself may give rise to strong and unprecedented feelings. Again, being in attendance is often a positive and powerful facilitator for grieving. At the bedside, beside the coffin, or at the cemetery, the reality of the event cannot be denied, yet there is still an opportunity to set right whatever wrongs may remain by sharing sentiments of forgiveness and caring.

Again, the child should be carefully prepared regarding what might happen at the moment of death or during a viewing of the remains. Grandma may not look "like herself" anymore. In the hospital, now, she may be too weak to speak. She may be expressionless. She may not be able to respond to touch or tears. In the casket, she may feel cold or look waxy. To the very young, it is appropriate to explain customs such as the half-couch coffin. It may even be a good idea to have a private viewing so that a parent could lift the lower portion of the coffin, proving to the child that the legs were not cut off so Grandma could fit into the box. At this time, the funeral director, clergyman, and parents could be available *just* to answer the child's other questions and to provide solace.

Exhibit 2 Child's Depiction of His Relationship with His Brother before and after the Brother's Illness

Rituals of the funeral service and expected behaviors of mourners can be explained. Grown-ups, too, can be silent, sad, and weepy. If adults are comforted by the structure, routine, and sense of closure that the rituals and burial or cremation afford, children should certainly be offered the same opportunity. Families may wish to hold a separate, short service for the children, or they may offer the children the option of attending any or every portion of the service or interment. To share a sense of loss in the comforting presence of their own family is a healthy, supportive way for them to learn how grief is eased in company.

A Chekov story, "Heartache," is the account of an old man desperately searching for someone to whom he can pour out his grief over his son's death. Thirsty to talk, separated by great distance from any living family, the grieving driver of a horse-drawn sleigh opens up to heedless strangers and indifferent passengers. The need to relive every painful detail with a sympathetic soul is so obvious to the old cabbie:

> He ought to tell how his son was taken ill, how he suffered, what he said before he died, how he died. . . . He ought to describe the funeral, and how he went to the hospital to fetch his son's clothes. (1947, p. 179)

Ultimately, the old man unburdens himself to the only one who will listen— his horse.

Brown (1955) has written a children's story in which youngsters deal with the mystery of death by sharing and repeating a ritual. Primarily a picture book, *The Dead Bird* is a tale of a group of children who conduct a funeral and burial ceremony as they have seen grown-ups do. They dig the grave for their little dead bird, sing songs, provide a marker and flowers, and visit the site with new offerings daily "until they forgot." "Until they forgot" is a crucial phrase; the process of reenacting the ritual allows them to put the event behind them and continue with their daily play.

Both for adults and for children, repetitions of word and ritual not only make the event real, but also ultimately grant it the necessary distance. There cannot be too many opportunities to retell or relive one's story, especially in the company of other caring souls. Company brings relief. It may be unbearably painful to evoke the image of a dead loved one when alone.

It is essential to help a child recall the happy and sad, or not so good, times with the deceased. Such a review of a relationship can ward off the unhealthy tendency to glorify or idealize the dead person. As Spender (1955) put it in "Double Shame,"

> At first you did not love enough
> And afterwards, you loved too much.

Youngsters are preoccupied with concerns that their bad words, misdeeds, or hostile feelings toward the dead person caused the disaster of death. Angry with Mommy, they may have cried out, "I hate you!" or wished the parent dead. Magical thinking and destructive fantasies must be eliminated.

It is not necessarily bizarre to suggest conversing with the dead. In Exhibit 3, a youngster is shown talking to his dead father through a photograph. He says his "I'm sorrys" and confesses his hidden guilts; then, changing seats,

Exhibit 3 Son's Depiction of a Conversation with His Dead Father

he responds to himself (or to his now empty chair) as he thinks his father would have responded.

Grief not properly faced can resurface unexpectedly. Individuals who use intense denial to protect themselves from expressing the sadness may break into violent weeping at relatively insignificant and totally unrelated events, or may even become physically ill. Again, in a role play scenario, a youngster explains to his classmate the dangers of unexpressed grief:

> The more you don't think of him, the sadder you'll get. Because in this place in the mind . . . (it's like water leaking out of a dam—if you don't stop it, it will leak out more and more until it will all come out and it will explode the dam). Well, that is sort of like a person. If you don't think of him, you'll get sadder and sadder and finally it all has to come out some way or other.

Parents should understand that children, like adults, need to grieve and that they may express their grief in different ways. One may be unable to cry; another may weep with vengeance. There may be a change in the child's eating and sleeping habits. A child may be unable to concentrate or may misbehave in school. One child may withdraw, while another pursues daily activities as if nothing had happened.

Words are not the only way to help youngsters and family members support one another through troubled times. As already indicated by the illustrations, children are quite comfortable with drawing and art modalities. They can mold or pound clay to depict how they feel about the death. A family may share the loss experience through separate sketches or collages, or through a family mural wherein each member shares a memory or association with the loss experience.

OTHER FACILITATORS FOR GRIEF

In the Chekov story, "Heartache," the horse who chews, listens, and breathes on her master's hand is the "therapist." The old man "is carried away and tells her everything" (1947, p. 180). A household pet is an invaluable ally for a child who has sustained a significant loss. Responding nonjudgmentally, the household animal appears totally accepting and adoring of the young master, who may cry or curse unabashedly.

The death of a pet, especially for a child, is a significant event not to be minimized by responses such as "Oh, it's only a dog." or instant replacement. Reviewing happy and sad times with the pet; assuring the child that the pet's death was not his or her fault, and that it is all right to feel sad, even angry, at the pet for "leaving;" and holding a funeral service as in *The Dead Bird* help the child work through the grief experience. The occasion of a pet's death can be used to teach children the dynamics of death and grief, as well as socially acceptable methods of expressing grief that contribute to emotional stability.

It is not necessary to wait for a tragedy to occur before the subject of death is raised. Parents may be well advised to set the stage and tone for dealing with crisis prior to a traumatic event. The following resources have been selected because of their appropriateness for family reading. Brief, inexpensive, and beautifully illustrated, they touch on a variety of losses with sensitivity and style:

- *The Fall of Freddie the Leaf,* Leo Buscaglia, New Jersey, Slack, 1982. Subtitled A Story of Life for All Ages, this book is about how Freddie and his companion leaves change with the passing seasons. It is only with the winter snow and his gentle fall from the branch that he comes to understand his part in the life of the tree, a knowledge that gives him pride and peace in his dying.

- *The Accident,* Carrol Carrick and Donald Carrick, New York, Clarion, 1976. Christopher blames the driver of the truck, then himself, for the death of his dog. He comes to realize that, no matter whom he blames, his dog will not come back. Nightmares and anger at his father are all part of working through his grief.

- *Tight Times,* Barbara Hazen and Trina Hyman, New York, Puffin, 1979. The loss of a father's job is a strain on this family.

- *Nona,* Jeffiner Bartole and Joan Drescher, New York, Harvey House, 1975. Through the grandson's eyes, the way in which a family copes with the immediate and long-term effects of a beloved grandmother's death is observed.

- *Talking about Death,* Earl Grollman and Gisela Heau, Boston, Beacon, 1970. The authors suggest the adult first becomes familiar with the contents, a dialogue between parent and child, and the Parent's Guide. With many suggestions for its use, the authors have provided a warm, calm account of the death of a grandfather and details that underscore how mourning is a necessary prelude to acceptance of the death.

Being in attendance when death happens, and discussing the subject with honesty, with openness, and with caring and concern, cannot prevent the birds of sorrow from flying overhead. But, to quote the ancient Chinese wisdom, it can prevent them from building nests in your hair.

REFERENCES

Adler, C. *We are but a moment's sunlight.* New York: Pocketbooks, 1976.

Anthony, S. *The child's discovery of death.* New York: Harcourt, 1940.

Bertman, S.L. "Death education: A primer for all ages." Unpublished manuscript, University of Massachusetts Medical School, Worchester, MA.

Bowlby, J. Processes of mourning. *International Journal of Psychoanalysis, 42,* 1966, pp. 418–438.

Brown, M.W. *The dead bird.* New York: Random House, 1955.

Chekhov, A. Heartache. In A. Yarnolinsky (Ed.), *The portable Chekhov.* New York: Viking Press, 1947.

Hoffman, H. *Struwwelpeter.* New York: Frederick Warne, 1944.

Hopkins, G.M. Spring and fall to a young child. In W.H. Gardner (Ed.), *Poems of G.M. Hopkins*. New York: Oxford University Press, 1967.

Hovey, Patricia. Manuscript verbatim. University of Massachusetts Medical School.

Kudret, C. Feast of the dead. In Adler & Stanford (Eds.), *We are but a moment's sunlight*. New York: Pocketbooks, 1976.

Nagy, M. The child's view of death. In H. Feifel (Ed.), *The meaning of death*. New York: McGraw-Hill, 1959.

Spender, S. The double shame. In *Collected Poems*. New York: Random House, 1955.

6. Interdisciplinary Care in Adolescent Bereavement

Bruce Conley
The Conley Funeral Home
Elburn, Illinois

In THE MINDS OF ADOLESCENTS, DEATH SELDOM EXISTS AS MORE THAN a concept in philosophy, a biology chapter about aging, or the surrealistic stuff of the latest horror movie. When it strikes, it pierces the blue skies of their world with the thundering impact of a lightning bolt.

As a funeral director, I have participated as a guest speaker in many classroom discussions about death and grief, and at times I have later walked with the same students to the casket of a classmate or parent. These experiences have spurred the educator in me to seek better ways to teach young people to deal with the emotional impact of the death of a friend or family member.

A TALE OF THREE TEENS

Philip was 16, but when his grandfather died, his mother was certain that Philip was much too "sensitive" a boy to be a pallbearer. "Philip has worshipped his grandfather since he was old enough to sit on his lap. They were very close . . . you can't even talk to Philip now. We usually just let him go out and get it off his chest. No, I'm sorry, but he's much too upset to take part in his grandfather's funeral. I don't know if he'll even be coming to the service."

Philip did come to the funeral, but neither his presence nor his grief were ever acknowledged. It was repeatedly said, however, that Philip had his grandfather's eyes. Of course, the big strapping man his grandpa was, he wouldn't want to see his grandson's eyes full of water! Philip would surely need to learn to be tougher if he was going to live up to his heritage.

It was assumed that because Philip was "a sensitive boy" he could not cope with the responsibility of performing the duty of pallbearer for his grandfather. This assumption denied Philip any opportunity of choice. It quietly underscored the family opinion that Philip's "sensitivity" was a weakness, something of an embarassment to the memory of his grand-father, whom he resembled so strongly in every other way. With no legitimate outlet for his grief and no acknowledgment of his individuality as a person, Philip obligingly made himself scarce throughout the funeral, allowing his mother to confirm her assessment of his character while mourning his absence at her side.

Laura was 14 when her best friend suffered a spontaneous brain hemorrhage and died on the volleyball court. She and Laura were fierce competitors. There was nothing they enjoyed more than to play against one another. Both had played exceptionally well that afternoon. Then, Marie had suddenly collapsed. Laura was inconsolable and wrapped herself in blame for the aggressive way she had spiked the ball at Marie that day.

In spite of her competitive nature on the court, Laura was a retiring person socially. With great difficulty, she attended the visitation at the funeral home. Over and over again, she tried to walk up to the open casket, but the very sight of her friend's blonde hair sent her retreating in tears to the door. No one really understood why Laura felt so very guilty. No one seemed able to help her say goodbye to her friend. No one seemed aware of her deep trouble until 6 months later when she dropped out of sports and then out of school.

Laura believed that she accidentally killed her best friend. She became both judge and jury and acted out her self-imposed sentence by sacrificing every talent she possessed and every evidence of success in her life. She not only convicted herself of involuntary manslaughter, but also sealed the verdict with her promise never to tell anyone how she really felt. She was convinced that no one could ever understand her and that everyone else blamed her for the tragic death of her best friend. The real tragedy was that she never could accept the biological facts of her friend's unpredictable and unavoidable death. To do so would have foiled her martyrdom. Strangely, it seemed more frightening to her to give up her feelings and talk about them than to give up her life as an athlete and a scholar.

John was 18 when his father shot himself. There was no question in the minds of relatives that John would become the "man of the house." He was 18, after all, and should be able to provide for his four younger brothers and sisters. Of course, his schooling would need to wait, but he didn't really want to go to college anyway. Maybe now that was a good thing; he was much too unsure of himself. He was also somewhat reclusive, the very image of his father in so many ways.

John was catapulted into the multiple roles of parent, provider, and supersibling almost before the obituary had published his name as the eldest surviving son. Perched on the very edge of manhood, he leaped into the work of raising his brothers and sisters and looking after his mother. With his uncles always there to advise him and remind him of his duty, he performed to levels that exceeded everyone's expectation, seemingly unaffected by the grief that surrounded his father's suicide. Paradoxically, as time went on, John found himself running away from his grief yet headlong into the perfect image of his father at 36, the age at which he died. In that year, John began to question whether the past would become the present and he would be compelled toward suicide by some inner force—a self-fulfilling prophesy.

Philip, Laura and John innocently fell heir to the precast roles of teenage grief outlined by the well-intentioned adults around them and by their own closed assumptions about themselves and their grief. The more serious impact of their experiences was not seen, however, until some months to years later when it was presented under the guise of another crisis. Typically, the family counselor in such later crises has no knowledge of the first and its relationship to the present problem. Similarly, the funeral director, clergy, and other medical, legal and emergency personnel involved with the original crisis are seldom aware of any effects they may have on later crises. An interdisciplinary approach to preventative intervention, involving communication among all individuals whose occupational roles bring them into contact with the adolescent over the course of bereavement, would do much to alleviate the problem.

INFORMATION/EDUCATION

When a death occurs in the family, adolescents are very likely to be privy to adult information and experience. Their deep desire to be treated as adults discourages them from asking questions, and their quiet facade is easily mistaken for understanding. Frequently, adolescents' accounts of a loved one's death reveal misunderstandings and inconsistencies concerning the time and place of accidents or the onset and course of a disease, and the cause and effect relationships among these events. Failure to discover and correct these misconceptions may foster a host of emotional complications. Laura's experience illustrates the importance of early and accurate clarification of the situational and biological course of events surrounding a death.

Educating adolescents and their families about grief from the earliest point possible is an important aspect of preventative intervention. While in periods of crisis this is seldom accomplished through direct teaching methods, many opportunities may occur for caregivers on all levels to explain and affirm the realities of grief; its roots, its normal course and healthy management. In Philip's case, both he and his parents were responding to folklore that the stifling of emotion is a sign of strength. While it is doubtful that the long family history could have been changed overnight, a simple acknowledgment of the appropriateness and necessity of Philip's tears could greatly have eased the burden of his grief.

Although adolescent life styles may appear to permit wide expression of almost any human emotion, open grieving and tears are still looked on as something to be avoided. Emotions related to exotic fantasy seem acceptable or tolerated but the genuine emotions of grief as a harsh reality of life remain something that is denied. Unaware of the normal course of grief or the danger of blocking its path, many adolescents make up their own game rules for grief and lock themselves into a collision course with emotional breakdown.

Lynch (1977) noted the apparently widespread view in the United States that human beings can rapidly form intimate relationships and then part with equal suddenness without anyone being hurt. A companion myth to this belief in "instant relationships" is the notion that any undesirable experience or emotion can be repressed out of existence, e.g., "If it feels good, do it; if it doesn't, ignore it until it goes away." Thus, even when good and thorough information is provided about the circumstances surrounding a death and the course of grief that must follow it, the social environment in which adolescents live may not permit them to use the information to their benefit.

COMMUNICATION

In the first case history, Philip's mother identified the most typical parental description of adolescent grief when she remarked, ". . . you can't even talk to him now. We usually just let him go out and get it off his chest." Like most adolescents, particularly males, Philip preferred his privacy and his peers to almost anything else. Caregivers who recognize this and seek to provide privacy and peer support for bereaved adolescents will soon gain for themselves the status of "trusted adult," which is another common need among bereaved adolescents.

Helping the adolescent secure some periods of privacy allows for a temporary detachment from the turbulence of the family's grief so that the adolescent can begin to isolate and deal with his own feelings. The sense of security resulting from such private times may also make the adolescent more receptive to the needs of the family. Similarly, when parents understand the adolescent's developmental task of separation and the related need for privacy, they may feel less rejected by the adolescent's independent behavior and therefore be more understanding.

Peer support brings the comfort of shared sorrow and an environment where the adolescent can feel on equal terms with others. The visitation or wake can help meet this same need for both adults and adolescents, but they must have their own space, and occasionally their own time. When there is an area of the funeral home facility that is somewhat secluded from the mainstream, it may be utilized as a gathering place for adolescents. While spontaneous gatherings will occur at other times and places, coming together at the funeral home allows the caregiver an opportunity to observe and occasionally to participate. Here too, the value of many physically poignant realities of death, such as the presence of the casket or perhaps photographs or memorabilia from the dead person's life, tend to make denial more difficult and can help focus conversation on the real reasons for having come together. Adapting to the private portion of the adolescent's search for answers, the caregiver may utilize self-help printed materials and other reading resources offered directly to adolescents or made conveniently available to them in the funeral home or other gathering environment.

Through various contacts with adolescents, caregivers who earn the role of adult confidant may be privileged to act as a sounding board for the adolescent's feelings. The caregiver may offer something of the wisdom of an adult and the companionship of a peer. In the absence of such a relationship, or in addition to it, the caregiver may offer skilled support to those who naturally act as peer-adult confidants in the adolescent's life.

From the point of bereavement crisis through the eventual approach to resolution, caregivers should be sensitive to adolescents varying needs to draw upon peer-support, understanding peer-adult relationships and personal opportunities for privacy. Efforts to identify and strengthen these resources while increasing parental awareness of them can be of great benefit.

PARTICIPATION

Participation is the kinetic principle of the funeral, which harnesses the emotional energies of grief to meaningful expression. From the decision making process of funeral arrangements to public involvement in the formal rites and ceremonies and private forms of creative expression, during and after the funeral, the goal of participation is to help the mourner transform the potential energies of emotion into kinetic energies of expression.

Unfortunately, except where the death of a peer is involved, most adolescents have little or no opportunity to express themselves when a family member dies. The funeral is essentially assumed to be an adult experience, which the adolescent may be allowed to witness but in which his participation may never be considered appropriate. It is the joint responsibility of caregivers, particularly during the funeral, to make adults aware of individual adolescent needs for self-expression or participation and to create appropriate opportunities for them to fulfill these needs.

Suggestions for adolescent participation include

- active participation: The adolescent may serve as pallbearer, honorary bearer, acolyte, lector, reader of the eulogy, or musician.

- passive participation: The adolescent may write an obituary or eulogy (to be read by someone else), or write a personal letter of unfinished concerns with the one who has died, or simply express personal remembrances. Mementos may be deposited in the casket as a symbol of completing the communication. The adolescent may make a floral arrangement or arrange a sharing table of memorabilia from the deceased's life.

- miscellaneous postfuneral activities: The adolescent may take part in the care of the gravesite or participate in the final disposition of the ashes, and may be involved in selecting the grave marker or monument or in creating or developing other memorials (tree plantings, plaques, photo albums, etc.), or choosing some of the dead person's personal belongings to keep.

While the funeral director normally bears responsibility for arranging and conducting the funeral, the facilitative efforts of associated caregivers (clergy, family counselors, social workers, etc.) who are aware of such participation possibilities can do much to help make them available to adolescents. The enormous need for self-expression in adolescents and in the bereaved family as a whole requires the cooperative sensitivities of all caregivers. Among such individuals in all professions, there is great need for concerned and ongoing communication from the time of bereavement through the funeral and follow-up.

APPROACHES TO PARTICIPATION

The following individual and group approaches to implementing the foregoing methods of involvement are adaptations of techniques which could be applied across a wide variety of situations. How appropriate or effective they may be will depend on the personalities of individual adolescents, the openness of the family as a whole, the internal and external dynamics of the death itself, and the sensitivities, time, and commitment of the caregivers.

Both the individual and group approach begin with a family conference involving as many members as possible (especially adolescents) and held as soon as possible after the death. The goal of this gathering is to cause the family to draw on whatever sense of unity may exist among them. Having called upon the family to make this commitment to each other, the caregiver may then begin to increase their awareness of each other as he identifies some of the individual needs that are likely to present themselves for adolescents as well as other family members. He may then suggest talking later with the adolescents individually or as a group, thus acknowledging the validity of their needs and expressing an intention to help meet those needs. The more traumatic the death, the more likely it is that the caregiver will witness an early and determined departure of adolescents from the family circle. While this is to be expected, and is a normal and often necessary reaction, the caregiver may have greater success with the family if they can be pulled together for this brief conference before the family becomes totally fragmented. Whenever possible, it is helpful to conduct such a conference with the joint support of the funeral director and clergy or counselor. This may help to balance discussion of emotional and spiritual needs with the practical realities of arranging and conducting a funeral to meet them.

Group Approach

The following case history was chosen to demonstrate the group approach both because of the uniqueness of the case and because of its universal attributes. It illustrates the flexibility of group involvement of adolescents.

A grandfather died suddenly, leaving eight grandchildren, nearly all of whom were in some way involved in the discovery of their grandfather's body and the calling of the emergency squad. After arrangements had been made with the parents and the needs of their children had been discussed, a gathering with the grandchildren (aged 9 to 18) was held in the home of the surviving grandparent (a place centrally located to all).

Initially, I asked each grandchild to share without interruption his or her version of what happened the day of their grandfather's death. I asked specifically where the child was when given the news, from whom he received it, what was said to him, how he felt as he heard the news, and what he most wanted to do or actually did at that time. The composite of all their responses clarified many details of the grandfather's death and seemed to relieve some undercurrents of scapegoating and guilt that had already begun to appear. The discussion of what happened at their grandfather's death gradually evolved into a recollection of his life. As both tears and laughter were brought forth, they were openly encouraged and acknowledged as necessary and appropriate. This fresh experience of emotion provided a natural setting for the discussion of grief and the value of mourning.

Returning to the recollection of their grandfather's life, I inquired what they would most want to do to honor the memory of their grandfather or to complete something they felt had been left unsaid or undone. I offered as examples the range of possibilities previously described. After some further discussion, they made their individual decisions, which were subsequently authorized by their parents.

The service was conducted with six pallbearers ranging in ages from 12 to 18, including two girls. Another child chose to play a piano piece for the funeral; still another to read a portion of the funeral ceremony from the established ritual of their faith. By the day of the funeral, most had placed something in the casket as their token of goodbye or as an expression of those things left unsaid or unfinished. On follow-up after the funeral (6 months and 1 year later) no adjustment difficulties were noted.

Although this particular set of circumstances would not often arise, it demonstrates the feasibility and the value of bringing the youth of the family together through participating roles within the funeral. Thus the goals of clarifying the facts of death, providing good grief education, and achieving some level of individual self-expression were accomplished.

While this type of group involvement of adolescents requires a great deal of time and coordination, its rewards can be considerable in terms of the positive experience it offers at a time when adolescents most need it. Group involvement not only assists the individual in learning to say goodbye, but also provides an important lesson in the healing experience of sharing one another's sorrow.

Individual Approach

Many deaths involve no more than one to three adolescent survivors whose special grief is often unintentionally overlooked. Betrayed by their adult-patterned behavior, they may especially be overinvolved in adult experiences and responsibilities that carry them beyond their capacity to cope. In contrast, their equally natural separatist behavior may cause them to be left alone and unsupported with no guidance.

Caregivers must be particularly aware of these characteristics in the lone adolescent who has no in-family peers with whom to share his grief and who has been overlooked as an "adult" by his parents. This adolescent may need to draw heavily on peer-adult relationships where they exist, or the companionship of the caregiver. When parents are distraught with their own grief and frequently showering more concern on younger siblings, the lone adolescent will likely be found seeking some privacy but yearning for understanding company. As the lone adolescent in the family, this child is frequently also the eldest child, sibling or grandchild of the deceased.

Accordingly, he or she will have a different remembrance or history of relationship than do younger siblings. As an individual in transition between child and adult, adolescents need the latitude to share at times as adults yet explore and express emotions on their actual level of development. The caregiver, as a third party observer, is often better positioned than parents to recognize the alternating needs of the adolescent in child/adult roles. Thus he may work to increase parental awareness of these roles, while indirectly modeling appropriate care as he seeks to assist the adolescent.

Inasmuch as the overall individual approach to adolescents is basically a person-to-person adaptation of the same techniques previously described in the group approach, it would scarcely appear to have deserved particular mention. Yet discussions with many who were "lone adolescents" in their family's first grief experience reveal that few perceived any special attention or guidance from any caregiver, aside from the tacit expectation that they "follow along." Thus the significant difference to be noted in the individual approach is more in recognition than in application. The powerful impact of grief often imprints indelible response patterns in adolescents, which guide them throughout their adult lives. Therefore particular attention to both group and individual adolescent needs is a significant and necessary acknowledgment of their unique place in the family system and an admonishment against the caregiver's unconscious neglect.

TIMING

That the days of crisis bring with them their own healing opportunities has been recognized in the wisdom of philosophers for centuries. Kliman (1978) noted that the ancient Chinese were aware of this, for in their language they combined the characters for *danger* and *opportunity* to create the ideogram for *crisis*. She stressed the value and appropriateness of situational crisis intervention, especially in the case of bereavement, in order to prevent the entrenchment of problems as part of the character of a stressed individual or family. She wrote, "If taken seriously at the moment of vulnerability, the danger or stress can be transformed into a healing, growth-promoting experience" (p. 12).

The importance of intervention in the early days of crisis, during which the funeral usually takes place, has been emphasized in the writings of a variety of other authors. Waldfogel and Gardner (1961), Rapaport (1965), and Kaffman (1965) contend that the family in crisis may be much more susceptible to the influence of "significant others" in the environment during this time. Klein and Lindemann (1961) stated that a maximum amount of change may be possible with a minimum of effort when contact is made with a family at the moment of crisis. Caplan (1961) asserted that families counseled in early crisis may be returned to a healthy path without analysis into the deep original reasons that made it difficult to handle a problem in a healthy way. Goldstein and Giddings (1973) concluded that "[a] little help, rationally directed and purposefully focused at a strategic time, may be more effective than extensive help given at a period of less emotional accessibility" (p. 195). Thus the overall value of early intervention seems clearly documented from many different sources and is noted particularly in bereavement crises.

INTERDISCIPLINARY COOPERATION

If research and study point toward more effective resolution of bereavement crises through early intervention, experience confirms as well the need for interdisciplinary cooperation among all bereavement caregivers, including medical emergency personnel, crisis line workers, counselors, clergy, funeral directors, physicians, nurses, coroners and medical/legal personnel as well as police. Kennedy (1977) has expressed it in these words:

> Our first line of response to troubled people cannot be provided by the relatively limited numbers of fully trained psychiatrists, psychologists, psychiatric social workers or marriage counselors. It must come from the persons who stand on the front line in whatever profession they find themselves. (p. vii)

Recognizing the need for broader professional awareness of family systems in bereavement, Bowen writes "[k]nowledge of family systems theory provides the professional person with a different dimension for understanding emotional interdependence and the long term complications of death in the family" (p. 335). Clearly, the complex family crises of our present day demand more coordinated interdisciplinary care. If this is to occur, especially in the area of bereavement crises, then much effort must be given to improving the level of education, communication and cooperation among all individuals whose occupational roles bring them into contact with bereaved persons regardless of the actual nature of their professional work. Adolescent bereavement is only one of the many areas of special need.

CONCLUSION

The ultimate success or failure of bereavement care for adolescents and the bereaved in general thus depends largely on the continuity of care in the delivery system. The silent role of caregiver must come to be identified as an inherent and integral part of the many different individuals whose lives and occupations touch bereaved persons of all ages. When ongoing communication among them is achieved, the level of continuity in emergency emotional care may then grow to parallel that of emergency medical care, where continuity has long been recognized as making the difference between life and death.

REFERENCES

Caplan, G. *An approach to community mental health*. London: Tavistock Publications, 1961.

Goldstein, S., & Giddings, J. Multiple impact therapy: An approach to crisis intervention with families. In G.E. Specter & W.L. Claiborn (Eds.), *Crisis Intervention*. New York: Human Sciences Press, 1973.

Kaffmann, M. Short-term family therapy. In H.J. Parad (Ed.), *Crisis intervention: selected readings*. New York: Family Services Assoc., 1965.

Klein, D.C., & Lindemann, E. Preventative intervention in individual and family crisis situations. In G. Caplan (Ed.), *Prevention of mental disorders in children*. New York: Basic Books Inc., 1961.

Kliman, Ann S. *Crisis: Psychological first aid for growth and recovery*. New York: Holt, Rinehart and Winston, 1978.

Lynch, James J. *The broken heart—The medical consequences of loneliness*. New York: Basic Books, Inc., 1977.

Rapaport, R. Normal crises, family structure and mental health. In H.J. Parad (Ed.), *Crisis intervention: selected readings*. New York: Family Service Association, 1965.

Waldfogel, S., & Gardner, G.E. Intervention in crisis as a method of primary prevention. In G. Caplan (Ed.), *Prevention of mental disorders in children*. New York: Basic Books, Inc., 1961.

7. Life-Threatening Illness in Youth

Robert M. Tull, M.D.
Kaiser-Permanente Medical Center
Hayward, California

Richard J. Goldberg, M.D.
Brown University Hospital
Providence, Rhode Island

WHEN AN ADOLESCENT HAS A LIFE-THREATENING ILLNESS, THE stress associated with normal emotional development and emergence into adulthood can be aggravated by feelings of loss of control, uncertainty about the future, and fear of bodily invasion. Those in the mental health field are beginning to recognize that adolescents facing life-threatening illness may frequently encounter severe problems with psychological development and social interaction. As advances in treatment methods have increased the number of children surviving such diseases as cancer, new problems are emerging for patients and their families. Koocher and O'Malley (1980), after examining the major effects of serious illness on ill adolescents and their families, developed a framework for interactions that may help in the development of coping strategies to overcome the psychological challenges posed by the disease.

New programs and services for patients, families, and health care professionals have sprung into existence across the country, and there has been an increasing interest in the fields of psychiatry, psychology, nursing, and social work in serious chronic illness in youth. This article addresses some of the common issues confronting seriously ill adolescents and children and their families.

BODY IMAGE

The development of body image is a major aspect of adolescence and is closely associated with the individual's self-concept. Adolescent body changes can be confusing for some, gratifying for others. Physical impairment limits freedom of movement and self-determination, as well as involvement in positive peer relationships.

Young patients facing a life-threatening illness frequently assess their physical limitations and emotional capabilities. Changes in these capabilities must be identified and addressed, because progress in living and continued psychological growth of sick adolescents depend on their abilities to engage in activities that provide them with continued satisfaction (Goldberg & Tull, in press).

Physical changes, brought about either by disease or by treatment, can be as subtle as lowered energy, or as dramatic as hair loss or amputation. Despite the physical limitations, however, adolescents must continue to increase their levels of control of themselves and their environment if they are ultimately to achieve autonomy (Erikson, 1950). Consequently, situations that interrupt the search for independence and success, particularly in

74

early and middle adolescence, are especially stressful to patients who are not able to reorient their objectives and goals (Hoffman, Becker, & Gabriel, 1973).

Parents must recognize that the loss of a body function, physical disfigurement, or lowered stamina are serious losses in and of themselves. These "minilosses" produce a reaction similar to a grief reaction to someone's death. The adolescent's emotional responses may include denial, anger, and depression. The family that feels and expresses their pain together is often able to assist the adolescent with alternatives that are more in tune with his or her physical abilities.

Understanding and recognition of physical limitations must be frequently assessed for the patient facing a serious illness. Therapists and parents can assist children by suggesting alternatives that are better suited to their physical abilities. One adolescent with Hodgkins disease said; "I used to ride my bike all the time, and I even used to race competitively occasionally. Now I lose energy much faster and get tired sooner, so I've had to cut back a lot. You know, you just have to know when to stop."

Despite the diagnosis of life threatening illness in adolescents it is important to continue to increase these young peoples' levels of control over themselves and their environment. It is important for families not to over protect patients, but to recognize the value for the child to continue to be active in other acceptable ways (Goldberg & Tull, in press). One 15-year-old girl with leukemia commented; "I've had to substitute things, like swimming and running for badminton and ping pong. . . I think it's just like redefining the activities I've chosen."

PEER GROUP

During early adolescence, peer group membership helps to bring about self-understanding and self-acceptance (Daniel, 1970). Independence and self-determination tend to be developed through the adolescent's social network. Therefore, despite potential problems with social and peer activity, the adolescent with a life-threatening illness should continue peer involvement in order to promote self-esteem and diminish fear of rejection and isolation.

Recent research suggests that adolescents with a serious illness who fail to complete appropriate developmental tasks may develop some permanent and irreversible maladaptive responses. In the largest group of survivors of childhood cancer studied thus far, Koocher found that nearly 50% of survivors had varying degrees of adjustment problems. In comparing those who cope successfully with those who do not, Koocher identified the most critical elements as problems with lowered self-esteem, lowered satisfaction with themselves, less ambition, and a greater gulf between the actual self and the idealized self (Koocher & O'Malley, 1980). One young 10-year-old diabetic child said, "It was like I was a piece of glass. Nobody wanted to get near me. They were all afraid I was going to break."

Peer groups among patients are becoming increasingly more important. These groups provide socialization and activity that might otherwise be lacking. A framework in which patients can express and ventilate their anxieties, reaffirm peer group acceptance through social and recreational activities, and assume independence and control through achievements in various programs can be extremely helpful. These groups can give the patient meaning through supportive, nonjudgmental give and take, while providing peer support (Goldberg & Tull, in press). Mutual experiences shared through peer groups can minimize feelings of depression and isolation as young people learn that others have similar reactions and feelings about their illness. Perhaps the greatest advantage lies in the fact that through the group process one helps oneself, and also enjoys the satisfaction of helping others. (Kaplan, 1981).

SOCIAL SUPPORT

Cobb (1976), in his review of the concept of social support, emphasized that a support system provides an individual with a sense of being a valued member of a network of people who share lines of communication and mutual obligations. Summarizing his 30 years of study in the area of psychological stress, Kaplan (1981) carried the analysis even further; he asserted that group support is a powerful tool with which the individual can master the potentially overwhelming effects of stress. Consistent with Mechanic's statement (1974) that "the ability of persons to maintain psychologial contact will depend not only on the intrapsychic resources, but also—and perhaps more importantly—on the social supports available or absent in the environment" (p. 32), it appears that effective social support is a crucial factor in the psychosocial adaptations to life-threatening illness (Goldberg & Tull, in press).

For most children and adolescents, supportive relationships and love provide the strength and structure for meeting the challenges of life and death. A cohesive family can be a refuge and source of strength during difficult times. Yet, traditional support structures have been disrupted through geographical mobility, decentralization of the family, and rising divorce rates. The rise of social programs in the 1960s and 1970s attests to the fact that institutions and agencies have assumed the supportive roles that were once the responsibility of family and community.

INTERVENTIONS WITH FAMILY

Family systems have a great deal of energy and potential power for change. Through the use of structural (Minuchin, 1974), strategic (Haley, 1973), and metaphorical techniques (Madanes, 1981), substantial change can be brought about relatively quickly. The family with an ill member does not consider itself a psychologically problematic family. Rather it is a unit into which a great deal of medical, emotional, and financial stress has been introduced. Therefore, interventions must be goal-directed, as brief as possible, and cost-effective.

Therapists who work with these families must understand systems. When a sick adolescent becomes an identified patient in family therapy, the larger family system and the more specific subsystems must be considered as well, siblings and the marital dyad also become patients (Kremer, 1981; Sourkes, 1980). It is important for a therapist not only to provide optimum care for the individual facing the life-threatening illness, but also to recognize when those who care for the patient need support. While the medical establishment is beginning to provide psychosocial support to the patient, very little has been done to address the needs of the family. Involving the family may be the most effective way to help the patient, however, since no professional can ever be as close to the patient as the family. It is the family that the adolescent relies on most in times of extreme crisis. Therefore, it is the therapist's task to help the family unit develop supportive techniques that allow the system to heal itself.

Tasks for the Family

To Be an Advocate for the Patient

The objectives of the medical system may not always be congruent with the adolescent's needs. Family members may find at times that their input provides important information. The therapist can assist the family in developing ways to communicate with the medical staff about side effects of treatments or symptoms when the patient is either in the hospital or at home.

Parents may need to represent their child's feelings about frequency of treatments, the need for further tests, when treatments are given, and even when to terminate treatment to the medical staff. Parents should strive to participate with their child and the medical staff in all such decisions. During these critical times, family values and involvement are more important than specific medical principles.

To Enhance the Patient's Autonomy

The loss of the sense of control is common in life-threatening illness and may contribute to the development of maladaptive behaviors. Helping an adolescent to maintain a sense of self-esteem and integrity throughout the experience of a serious bodily assault can be an important task of the family. On an interpersonal level, verbal or nonverbal communication that the patient is loved and valued provides major support. In addition, it is important to give the patient a sense of continued mastery in daily activities. One therapist taught a family the relaxation exercises that helped a young cancer patient decrease his nausea and vomiting during chemotherapy. The entire family benefited from the instruction and began meditating together on a daily basis.

To Maintain Social Support

At times, because of their own increased anxiety and distress, relatives and friends may avoid visiting the seriously ill patient. The therapist can help the family develop ways of interacting with these relatives and friends in a manner that reduces their anxiety and increases contact between the patient and his or her friends.

> One 14-year-old boy with cancer was going to return to school after 4 months of chemotherapy. He was extremely concerned about the reactions of his peers and his teachers when he walked onto the playground after all that time away. Fortunately, his two siblings were in the same school. In a family session, the therapist created role plays to help the siblings find ways to inform the other children and staff about the patient so that they would not respond to the returning boy as a "freak." It greatly enhanced the young patient's return to school and allowed the siblings to feel that they could help their brother.

To Encourage Communication

Among the characteristics that help a family adjust to serious illness is direct and consistent communication (Olsen, 1970). In one study, family members' perceptions of communication in late stage cancer were examined. Intrafamilial communications regarding illness and dying were frequently discordant and guarded leading to perceptions that the patient was withdrawing. More than half the family members reported they were uncomfortable when visiting the patient and experienced feelings of helplessness (Krant & Johnson, 1977–1978). Communication breakdowns within the nuclear and extended family often come about when one member withholds or distorts information about another. Often parents decide (nearly always incorrectly) that certain things should be withheld from the sick adolescent. Such a decision often creates a distance between parent and adolescent, and the isolation resulting from this communication dysfunction increases stress among the family.

Fears about the patient's deterioration and pain can result in withdrawal from the patient because of the family's anxiety about impending disaster. Therapists can encourage the family to examine interactional and informational difficulties and create new ways to deal with problems. They can have the family "practice" open discussion in the sessions and illustrate that expressions of grief and fear can be constructive in keeping a family "feeling" together.

Family Difficulty in Providing Support

The therapist who engages the family in counseling can gently elicit affect while respecting the individual's style of coping. The stress of the family of a young patient can be overwhelming. "What can I do? I feel helpless. I feel like I'm going crazy. What will happen to me?" These are common concerns. It is important to try to understand what is happening when family members appear to be having difficulty fulfilling their roles.

There are four important issues that staff should be alerted to when trying to understand reasons families are having problems in providing support.

1. The family may have to change its life style. For example, one parent may have to quit a job to care for the sick patient. Parents may also become isolated from their own friends and resources, thus losing their own social support system.
2. Family members might find themselves maintaining a balance between a desire to remain vitally involved in the child's life and treatment, and a desire to protect themselves against the horrible pain of the child's death by distancing themselves from the child psychologically. When a child or adolescent is confronted with a life-

threatening illness, anticipatory grieving may start immediately. The family may keep a fluctuating distance to prepare for the eventual loss.
3. Some families find themselves overwhelmed by the recurrence of past grief. This rekindled grief may interfere with their interactions with the patient.
4. A family member might develop his or her own depressive reaction, confusion, and stress-related syndrome.

Families bring their own individual background and experience to the illness situation. The family must be viewed as a group of individuals with unique histories that will in part determine their capability for involvement in the treatment process. Many families of children with life-threatening illness encounter difficulties with relationships, affective responses and communication with which they might be helped by a family therapist. The foremost goal of the therapist is creation and maintenance of a relationship in which the family can better deal with the stresses, challenges, and supportive tasks involved with caring for a child with a life-threatening illness.

Unfortunately life is too complex to allow for the development of a simple recipe that one might follow to enhance a family's ability to cope with serious illness. Individual needs of the young patient and the family, as well as the unique characteristics of the relationships and the situation, make for a large number of possible variables. No one rule is right for everyone. However, the issues raised in this chapter may help therapists gain some perspective concerning the problems facing the family and patient as one very special system.

REFERENCES

Cobb, S. Social support as a moderator of life stress. *Psychosomatic Medicine,* 1976, *38,* 300–312.

Darrell, W.A. *The adolescent patient.* St. Louis: Marby, 1970.

Erikson, E. *Childhood and society.* New York: Norton, 1950.

Goldberg, R.J., & Tull, R.M. *The psychosocial dimensions of cancer: A Practical Guide for Health Care Providers.* New York: The Free Press, in press.

Haley, Jay. *Uncommon therapy: The psychiatric techniques of Milton H. Erickson.* New York: Norton, 1973.

Hoffman, A., Becker, R.D., & Gabriel, P.H. *The hospitalized adolescent: A guide to managing ill and injured youth.* New York: The Free Press, 1976.

Kaplan, G. Mastery of stress: Psychological aspects. *American Journal of Psychiatry,* 1981, *138,* 4, 413–420.

Koocher, G.P., & O'Malley, J.E. *The Damocles syndrome: Psychosocial consequences of surviving childhood cancer.* New York: McGraw-Hill, 1980.

Krant, M.J., & Johnson, L. Family members' perceptions of communications in late stage cancer. *International Journal of Psychiatry in Medicine,* 1977–1978, *8,* 203–216.

Kremer, R.F. Living with childhood cancer: Healthy siblings perspectives. *Issues in Comprehensive Pediatric Nursing,* 1981, 155–165.

Madanes, C. *Strategic family therapy.* London: Jossey-Bass, 1981.

Mechanic, D. Social structure and personal adaptation: Some neglected dimensions. In C.V. Coelho, D.A. Hamburg, & J.E. Adams (Eds.), *Coping and adaptation.* New York: Basic Books, 1974.

Minuchin, S. *Families and family therapy.* Cambridge, MA: Harvard University Press, 1974.

Olsen, E.H. The impact of serious illness in the family system. *Postgraduate Medicine,* 1970, *47,* 169–174.

Sourkes, B. Siblings of the pediatric cancer patient. In J. Kellerman (Ed.), *Psychological aspects of childhood cancer.* Springfield, IL: Charles C. Thomas, 1980.

8. Helping Children Cope with a Sibling's Death

J. Donald Schumacher
Somerville, Massachusetts

THE STUDY OF DEATH AND BEREAVEMENT AND THEIR EFFECTS ON human development are receiving a good deal of attention in the current psychological literature. Kubler-Ross (1969) outlined for the general population a model that describes how human beings cope with death. This model joined the theories of the grieving process that were already being developed within traditional psychology. Until this time, the realities of death and bereavement frequently were shrouded in a "conspiracy of silence" and were dealt with only in private. Individuals preferred to avoid the reality until death became a matter of personal experience either through their own impending death or that of a loved one. Even then, the resources for effective coping were limited to religion, the nuclear family, and perhaps a few friends. Few sought help or shared their grief elsewhere unless the loss caused a severe psychiatric problem.

Although little was being said about death, even less was being said about bereavement and its far-reaching effect on development. Freud made his first references to the pathological repercussions of an individual's struggle to mourn the loss of a loved one in "Mourning and Melancholia," published in 1917. While the individuals studied by Freud were extreme in their pathology, it can be seen from this work that unresolved loss can lead to a constant search for the recovery of the lost object that leaves the individual in a continually depressed state.

Clearly, it takes a tremendous effort to deal with death. While grieving is a normal process, adjustment to such a loss draws on the most sophisticated skills of the individual's psychology. Operating from this framework, it would seem that, as difficult as it is for adults to comprehend the import of the loss, children are at an even greater psychological disadvantage, being less developed in their cognitive ability to understand the meaning of death.

REVIEW OF THE LITERATURE

It is clear that parental death is a primary object loss for the child and causes a conscious mourning behavior. Bowlby (1963) hypothesized that this primary loss also results in an often undefined, aimless yearning and searching for the lost object that extends into adult life. Variables such as the child's age at the time of the parent's death, family constellation, holding environment (the nurturing surroundings that foster or inhibit growth), and the reactions of the remaining parent all affect the child's ability to come to terms with the loss (Barnes, 1960; Bowlby, 1968).

83

Although a good deal has been written on the child's reactions to the loss of a parent, the effect of childhood sibling death and its influence on development was largely ignored until the mid-1940s. One of the first studies on the effects of sibling death was done by Rosenzweig and Bray (1943). In a series of interviews with schizophrenic patients, they found that one or more sibling deaths had occurred during the early development of these patients. Although the number of patients was limited and the true meaning of these deaths was unclear to the researchers, they felt that the losses had a potential causal relationship to the problems besetting the patients. They called for more research into the possibility that sibling loss was a major contributing factor in the illnesses of both schizophrenic and other psychotic individuals.

The task of childhood mourning over a sibling is related to the child's age, the child's perception and awareness of the meaning of death, the ways in which the parents cope with the loss, and the nature of the sibling relationship before the death (Vernon, 1970). A child's grieving over a lost sibling is frequently overshadowed by the intense reaction of the parents. The remaining children are often forgotten; the loss of a child is such a trauma for the parents that most of the immediate attention goes to them. Thus, childhood mourning often goes underground, either forever or until a time later in life when it can be expressed without fear that it will further hurt the parents (Lieberman, 1979).

Surviving siblings, then, are often afterthoughts that are dealt with in a variety of ways. Lieberman (1979) noted that sometimes family members attempt to help the siblings by ''protecting'' them from the realities of death with philosophical and religious speeches, preventing them from seeing the body, or by making up stories about the death to shield them from any real or imagined guilt connected to the loss. Shielding often backfires and highlights for children any sense of guilt or responsibility that they may feel, however. Many parents are advised not to tell the remaining children all there is to know about the death on the theory that the knowledge will upset the children and make the incident remain longer in their minds (Cain, Fast, & Erickson, 1963). This reaction by the parents is understandable, as many of them feel so overwhelmed by the loss that they fear their children will also be overwhelmed and will be even less able to handle it than they are. In addition, parents fear that, because of their own grief, they will be unable to handle one or more extremely upset children. Rosen and Cohen (1981) argued that avoidance is exactly the wrong thing to do. Children kept from the realities of the death make up their own fantasy of what happened and whose fault it was, and they begin to wonder whether they will be next to slip away into that world where no one remembers them or talks about them anymore.

In many cases, the remaining children and at least one of the parents blame themselves for the death (Cain et al., 1963). For the children, the fact that Johnny was perceived as the favored child or the better athlete results in the development of a normal sibling rivalry, which is often played out in fantasy by wishing the envied sibling to be dead. The fantasy is a way of exerting power over an ambivalently hated object, as well as a way to receive the kind of parental attention desired. It is generally not connected to any real understanding of the permanence of death. If this wishing is followed by the real death of the sibling and the incredible upheaval in the family, the uncomprehending child is left stunned by the act he or she has "committed." While most children handle such guilt within the framework of their own personality structure, they observe and often duplicate the coping style of their parents. Cain, Fast, and Erickson catalogued the frequent child reactions as "depressive withdrawal, accident prone behavior, punishment seeking, constant provocative testing, exhibitionistic use of guilt and grief, massive projection of super ego accusations and many forms of acting out" (1963, p. 743).

Krell and Rabkin (1979) hypothesized that three types of children emerged from the families who participated in conspiracies of silence as a result of guilt, the all-consuming importance of the remaining children, or the need to substitute one of the remaining children or a new birth for the dead child: the haunted child, the bound child, and the resurrected child. Haunted children are those who live in fear of what may happen to them. The facts about the death of their sibling have been withheld from them because of the guilt and shame their family feels for the dead child. These children become the caretakers of their parents' feelings and are constantly vigilant lest they remind their parents of the dead child. While they participate in the silence at home, they frequently misbehave in school or develop severe phobias and somatic symptoms.

Bound children are overprotected because their parents live in dread that they may lose another child. Their real and imagined fears lead to the development of a new family system that is closed, guarded, overprotective, and restrictive. Children in this system are prevented from being the normal, inquisitive, and risk-taking beings that other children are. This system often causes the children to withdraw into an angry world occupied only by themselves, their fearful parents, and the ghost of their dead sibling to remind them of what they are not allowed to experience. Angry behavior and, ultimately, rejection of the parents are common among these children.

Resurrected children are seen as substitutes for their lost sibling. These children are treated as though they were the dead child. Their chance of establishing identities of their own is very slim, as their parents consistently undermine their attempts to develop a unique personality. This can cause severe personality disorders, as well as more serious psychotic behavior.

Unconscious guilt can be a prime mover in an individual's method of coping with loss and organizing later personality and adult relationships, as shown in the following case presented by Berman (1978).

A patient's infant sister had died when he was 3 years old. Her death was followed by an overprotected relationship with his mother, in which he was told that his sister's death occurred so that his mother would be able to give all her attention to him. This man was unable to tolerate the intimacies of his later interpersonal relationships. During the process of analysis, he remembered his death wishes for his sister and his belief that he had killed her to remain close to his mother. In his subsequent relationships, he had always felt afraid to become too close to women and yet was devastated when the relationships ended, feeling that he was totally responsible for their termination and that he had done something that was tantamount to murder.

The loss of a sibling affects the family system and the individual children in many ways. The circumstances of the death itself, the reactions of the parents, the relationship of the siblings before the death, and the parental ability to help the remaining children deal with the death all determine how the siblings will be able to mourn their loss. It would seem that not only is the surviving child's personality development affected, but also the ability to form and maintain future healthy relationships.

THE SURVIVING SIBLING'S PERSPECTIVE

In interviews with 15 bereaved families conducted by this author in 1982, the surviving siblings, all between the ages of 9 and 13, reported several major concerns. These themes hold true regardless of the type of death that has occurred (e.g., from cancer, suicide, or accident).

The first concern is their need for direct communication. Unless parents and other adults are as open and honest about the death as possible, the children must find their own answers to questions that are often beyond their comprehension. Not only does parental sharing of the facts help the siblings to incorporate the realities of the death, but also it links the children to an emotional part of the parent that they are afraid of losing.

Siblings also need permission to share their very changeable feelings. Many siblings feel that they cannot share the anger and resentment they feel toward the lost sibling because they are afraid of hurting or being rejected by their parents. Many children are angry with the dead sibling for the uproar that the child has caused or the pain they see their parents experiencing. Overprotectiveness can cause children to be angry with both their parents and their dead sibling. They are angry with the sibling for dying and "making my parents smother me," and they are angry with their parents for not seeing that they are different from their sibling and that they want to live like normal children. This anger is often balanced by the sadness they themselves feel over the loss. They are confused because they experience many conflicting emotions simultaneously. Parental encouragement and sharing of their own feelings can enable the children to express these feelings as a normal part of their grief.

Guilt is difficult for most siblings to identify and understand. Many siblings feel responsible for the death because of a fight they had with the sibling before the death or because of an historically conflict-filled relationship. As mentioned earlier, wishing their sibling dead or out of the way is a common way for children to resolve a difficult relationship. Many children feel that this wish caused the death of their sibling, despite reassurances from the parents. These children frequently wish that it had been they and not their sibling who died. This is their way of trying to redeem themselves for having "caused" the death.

"What do I tell my friends?" is a question of supreme importance to many siblings. Frequently, siblings feel that their friends do not understand what they are experiencing. Attempts to share the import of the loss may be met with blank stares and quizzical looks. Because their friends often do not know what to say to them or do not want to be reminded that they, too, could lose a sibling, children who have lost a sibling frequently find themselves avoided by old friends. Consequently, the bereaved sibling may feel rejected, isolated, and, at times, even freakish. They may feel unable to play with their friends at old games in which death played a primary role. School can become a painful experience, and many siblings find ways to avoid attending classes.

Often, siblings are afraid to establish a new life without the sibling. They fear that being happy again or going forward in their lives will suggest to others that they did not care about their dead sibling or, perhaps worse, will indicate that they really did not care. They are concerned about showing too much happiness in front of their parents for fear that their parents will become sad or rejecting or will think that the remaining children do not need as much of their parents' attention as they do.

Another concern is that of losing other important people or pets to death. Many children report that they were fairly unaware of death or accidents before the death of their sibling. After the death, they become fearful that their parents or other siblings will die and exhibit oversolicitous behavior toward them. This fear of another loss causes a high level of anxiety that may be revealed in sleeplessness, loss of appetite and/or obsessive eating, failing grades, and a generally fearful existence.

Holidays are a time of sadness for the entire family. Many siblings feel especially confused at this time because they would like to participate in the joy of the holiday, but they feel sad at the same time. They want to remember their sibling; yet it causes pain to do so. Some children feel angry with their dead sibling for "ruining" the holiday time. This ambivalence is often accompanied by guilt about and fear of forgetting their dead sibling.

It is clear that grieving over a sibling is a complicated process that challenges even the most mature children. Parental reactions, conflicting feelings, guilt, lack of understanding, sadness, anger, and fear all contribute to the siblings' struggle to understand what has happened to them.

TREATMENT

In therapy with bereaved siblings and their families, it is necessary to address the individual personalities of the children, as well as their relationships to each other, the dead sibling, and their parents. This requires an approach that can identify not only the roles and alliances within the family, but also the problems that have developed as a result of the death.

Anticipated Death

Long-term illness has a unique set of dynamics that begins as soon as the child becomes ill. At that point, a significant amount of parental energy is focused on the ill child. This begins for the other children in the family a long road not only of watching their sibling grow weaker and die, but also of watching their parents become more and more focused on the impending loss. This creates in the family a sense of imbalance in that people change, roles reverse, and family security is felt to be in serious jeopardy. As the parents deal with the illness, so do the children. If parents are actively communicating with each other and their children, the siblings will be better able to share their fears and concerns about the changes that they are experiencing. If, however, parents are unable to speak honestly about the loss, the children will become more fearful and isolated in that fear.

A therapist coming into this situation must be aware that emotions, while perhaps not being talked about directly, are keenly felt and are just below the surface levels of communication. Frequently, the pain of the family members is clearly seen in their faces or in somatic complaints. The children may be very aggressive, exhibiting a great deal of acting out behavior, or they may be severely withdrawn. Again, this is often modeled after the behavior of the parents.

Therapy, then, must begin slowly. The participation of the ill child who is central to the process of letting go and change that is taking place may be encouraged. This child is often left out because the parents feel that the child is "too ill" or that it will be "too much" for the child. This is, of course, frequently a projection of the parents' fear that it will be too much for themselves. While it is inappropriate to mandate this child's attendance, the importance of the ill child's presence may be explained to the parents in terms of the child's key role in the changing family. Parents are also able to see the necessity of the child's participation when the feelings of isolation and separateness of the ill child are addressed during the treatment.

In the first sessions, it is not necessary to deal with death. The prime issues are the changes that are taking place in the family because of the illness. A good starting place is to have all members draw a picture of the family. This serves the dual purpose of breaking the ice and of diagnosing the various levels of awareness about the illness, the changing family structure, and the impending death. The therapist must then decide how much work is to be done within the structure of family therapy and how much should be done in other settings. For example, it may become clear that the major source of problems in the family is not the illness itself, but the relationship of the couple. It may be impossible for the family to restructure itself if the couple is badly disorganized or filled with guilt. It may become important, then, for the therapist to meet with the couple alone and also as a part of the family.

Through drawings, children are able to communicate their true feelings and perceptions about what is happening in their world. They may be reluctant to discuss their drawings in front of their parents and siblings, either because of their personality or because of their fear of hurting their parents or ill sibling. The therapist can facilitate the process of sharing by meeting in a grouping that is comfortable for the children, such as all the siblings, some of the siblings and a parent, or a child individually. This approach allows each child to talk freely about his or her drawing.

In the discussion of drawings and feelings, the entire family should be brought to understand that the things they are experiencing are normal and that other families in similar situations feel the same emotions. This helps to reduce the sense of freakishness that is often felt and to foster a normalcy that is feared lost. Once the children have learned that what they have to share in their drawings is not atypical for the situation, it is important to bring the entire group together to discuss the drawings again as a family.

Having laid the rough groundwork by the discussions of each person's drawing, the therapist can facilitate the ongoing dialogue about both the changing family structure and the approaching death. The children should be encouraged to continue to share their needs, as they tend to withdraw into noncommunicative behavior as the pain of the loss grows more dramatic. The parents should be encouraged to share their feelings of sadness, anger, and helplessness, as it helps the children to realize that they are all experiencing similar emotions. In effect, the therapist is creating a safe place where the grief can begin.

The dying child is of paramount importance in this process. It is incumbent on the therapist to assess continually the ill child's ability to be a part of the process. Most dying children want to participate, as they want to continue as a full-fledged member of the family. In addition, these children are extremely aware of the disorganization caused by their illness. They, too, feel guilty for the pain their illness is causing their parents and siblings. Being a part of the treatment enables them to feel that the family is fighting this illness together and helps to eliminate some of the isolation that is felt as a part of dying.

Dying children are acutely aware of the feelings that their siblings are directing—or not directing—toward them. If children can share their emotions with their dying sibling, a forum is established for normal sibling communications: competition for parental attention; feelings of anger, sadness, and grief; the resolution of historically unfinished business; and plans for the dissemination of articles owned by the dying child. This last is crucial in order to alleviate any guilt siblings may feel for enjoying anything that had belonged to the dying child and enables the dying child to continue to be a part of his or her sibling's life.

As the death looms closer, it may be impossible for the dying child to be a part of the therapy. In this case, the therapist must work with the children and their parents to develop a time, place, and way to say goodbye. Many parents and surviving children become disconnected as death nears. The parents spend a great deal of time with their dying child. Siblings may feel the loss of both their parents and their brother or sister. Including the surviving children in a well-timed goodbye can do much to reduce their anxiety about the loss, give them some closure on the death, and keep them connected to their parents.

After the death, it is important to continue to meet with the entire family as a new unit. The number of sessions needed depends on the amount of unfinished business within the family. Therapy can serve as a forum for grieving, as well as for airing problems that arise in defining the new system. If the therapy has been successful, the surviving children will feel that they can use the sessions to ask for any assistance needed in confronting their parents with both their pain and their needs. The therapist has served as a temporary "parent" to both the children and the parents as they struggled to find direction and support during the dying process. Now, the therapist must ensure that the couple has enough strength to manage their new system and gradually return the role of parent to them. The process of treatment has enabled them all to grieve in a safe system that provided some boundaries while their family felt out of control.

Sudden Death

Sudden death catches family members unprepared, with unresolved issues. In the case of an anticipated death, including the dying child in the therapy can help the family to resolve their issues before the death occurs, but sudden death often exacerbates those very issues. Bereaved children whose siblings die suddenly are often left with an incredible sense of guilt over unresolved issues between them and their sibling or their parents. This sense of guilt, coupled with the feelings of grief, causes emotional isolation. The parents, feeling ultimately responsible for their children's well-being, withdraw over their "failure" and fear that they will "fail" again. The siblings then struggle alone with guilt and anger, feeling that they have lost their parents as well as their brother or sister.

It generally takes a while for families to realize that they are in trouble. Sometimes it takes weeks; often it takes years. Parents may try almost any means to avoid dealing directly with the pain and guilt: having another child, overindulgence and/or overprotectiveness of the surviving children, and divorce, to name a few. The therapist entering this system is faced not only with the grief, but also with new dynamics that have been added to the family before the old ones have been sorted out. Misbehavior, depression, overly solicitous behavior, overeating, and perhaps self-destructive acts are often exhibited by the children. These are generally representations of the modeled parental behaviors motivated by guilt, fear, and blame.

Initially, it is important to talk with the couple about how their reactions to the death of their child are affecting their surviving children. The next step is to include the children in the sessions, again using drawings to clarify both their perceptions of the family and their relationship with the dead sibling. Using this information, the therapist attempts to discuss with the family the circumstances surrounding the death, including the actual cause of death and the unresolved relationships that existed before the death. Such discussions enable the therapist to see who's blaming whom and, through the process of therapy, to remove the blocks placed in the way of grieving.

Often the guilt, blame, and overreactions on the part of both the children and the parents have made it impossible for them to face the true import of the loss. An open discussion not only clarifies facts and unresolved issues, but also promotes resolution of the guilt and mutual support. If the parents are unable to let go of the guilt and the blame, it is unlikely that the siblings will be able to do so. In this case, it is vital to treat the couple separately while continuing the family therapy. Frequently, the therapist finds that there is a history of unresolved conflicts between the couple and that the death has become the scapegoat for years of feeling helpless to change a difficult marriage. If the couple can resolve their preexisting conflicts through treatment, both the family system and the ability of its members to grieve will improve. If not, the process of grief frequently gives way to the process of marital separation.

As the parents are working through their conflicts, the therapist should address any feelings of responsibility that exist among the children. These children may blame themselves for their parents' problems, or they may blame their siblings, both alive and dead. The parents need to share the process of their conflict resolution with the children, as it will facilitate the children's ability to separate the issues of death and marital disharmony, as well as to understand their real responsibilities in each.

When the parents are able to separate their marital problems from the problems caused by the death, the entire family can discuss the death, determine its meaning to each member, and define the new family. The therapist can most help the siblings by providing them with a safe place in which to express their fears about the death and perhaps about their parents' troubles without taking responsibility for them. Again, the therapist acts as a temporary ''parent'' until the parents can resume their total roles; this allows the children to maintain an emotional connection to an adult who shares with them the truth about the problems in their family, gives them the facts about the death, and provides support for their expression of their feelings about the family, their parents, and themselves.

Goals of Therapy

The role of the therapist is to act as a grief facilitator. The therapist must work to help each family member grieve in his or her own way within the family unit. By dispelling the myth that the less a child knows, the better, and by promoting open and honest sharing of the many feelings associated with the death of a child, the therapist helps maintain a functional family system.

Siblings are best helped by an adult who answers their questions as directly as possible. Therapy can provide an environment in which questions and fears can be addressed. In either anticipated or sudden death, it is important to address the role of the dead child in the family system. In addition, the medical facts of the child's death should be shared with the siblings so that destructive fantasies regarding responsibility for the death can be prevented.

Clarifying the relationship between the couple facilitates the siblings' ability to mourn by improving the grieving behavior modeled by the parents. Should the relationship of the couple dissolve in separation or divorce, therapy enables the siblings to divest themselves of responsibility in the dissolution of the marriage.

Most importantly, therapy can enable a child to "let go" of a dead sibling and integrate the memories of the sibling without integrating the guilt and feelings of responsibility.

REFERENCES

Barnes, M.F. Reactions to the death of a mother. *Psychoanalytic Study of the Child*, 1960, *15*(9), 52.

Berman, L.E.A. Sibling loss as an organizer of unconscious guilt: A case study. *Psychoanalytic Quarterly*, 1978, *47*(4), 568–587.

Bowlby, J. Pathological mourning and childhood mourning. *Journal of the American Psychoanalytic Association*, 1963, *11*, 500–541.

Cain, A.C., Fast, I., & Erickson, M.E. Children's disturbed reactions to the death of a sibling. *American Journal of Orthopsychiatry*, 1964, *34*, 741–752.

Freud, S. Mourning and melancholia. *Standard Edition*, London: Hogarth Press, 1957. (Originally published, 1917).

Krell, R., & Rabkin, L. The effects of sibling death on the surviving child. *Family Process*, 1979, *10*, 471–477.

Kubler-Ross, E. *On death and dying.* New York: Macmillan Press, 1969.

Lieberman, F. *Social work with children.* New York: Human Sciences Press, 1979.

Rosen, H., & Cohen, H. Children's reactions to sibling loss. *Clinical Social Work Journal,* 1981, *9*(3), 211–219.

Rosenzweig, S., & Bray, D. Sibling deaths in the anamneses of schizophrenic patients. *Archives of Neurology and Psychiatry,* 1943, *49*, 71–102.

Vernon, G.M. *Sociology of death.* New York: Ronald Press, 1970.

9. Professional Stress: Adaptation, Coping, and Meaning

Marcia E. Lattanzi
Boulder County Hospice
Boulder, Colorado

FAMILIES ENTER A TIME OF ACUTE CRISIS AND DYSFUNCTION WHEN they are anticipating or have experienced the death of one of their members. The tasks of maintaining adaptive resources and reestablishing levels of well-being for families dealing with death and grief are extremely difficult ones. Therapists who work with families during these times experience stresses that are similar to and reflective of the families' difficulties. In addition, therapists are reminded of their own past and future losses and become more aware of their own vulnerability.

Death creates a basic conflict in our lives. People operate in their relationships with the belief that there will always be more time: more time to correct misunderstandings, more time to love people, more time to communicate that which has been unexpressed. Family therapists enter a moment in the family's life when pain and conflict are the dominant experiences. To some degree, human beings are withdrawn and inconsolable at these times. The usual therapeutic intervention with families involves defining goals by asking questions related to their needs and examining individual experiences. Death and grief force family members into uncharted territory, however. A family therapist who is challenged to explore this unknown area with the family must be an approachable, secure guide with a good sense of timing for the journey.

GOALS AND ISSUES

Family therapists know well the biological principle that adaptation is basic to survival. Individuals dealing with grief, whether because of their own impending death or because of the death of a loved one, all sustain emotional assaults on their ego (Pattison, 1978). The general therapeutic goal of helping individuals and families attain the best level of health and functioning possible is complicated by the dysfunction inherent in grief. It is not possible to deal "reasonably" with what is very often an unreasonable life situation (Garfield, 1978). While change is usually the object of family therapy, undesired changes have already been imposed on the family in situations of death and grief. Roles are shifting, and family members are struggling to redefine their lives. In small families (two to four members), role adjustments are likely to be even more difficult because there are fewer options for shifting within the family. The family therapist becomes involved in the situational distress and frustration experienced by the family as they struggle to adapt.

In an evolutionary sense, families existed to offer a degree of safety and protection from predators. There is an almost instinctive human desire to nurture and protect those that we love. Death and grief make us face our powerlessness, our inability to keep our loved ones safe from painful experiences. This reality is complicated by the fact that each family member is suffering and cannot fulfill contracts of mutual support, even when family members have close relationships. One of the significant stresses involved in work with families around issues of death and grief is a recurring sense of helplessness or irreversibility, which usually reflects the strain and emotional dysfunction of the family.

SITUATIONAL CONFLICTS

Families experience specific stresses that are involved in the experience of an impending death, and in the aftermath of a loved one's death.

Physical and Environmental Stresses

The basic operational patterns of individuals and families are disturbed prior to and following a death. If a family member is suffering from a debilitating terminal illness, problems associated with physical deterioration, lack of energy, demands and effects of the treatment process, and assumption of the ill person's roles and responsibilities emerge. A family therapist may need to keep sessions brief and to schedule them around the changes in routine and demands placed on family members. It is often difficult for all members of the family to attend a session. When the ill person is hospitalized, the reactions of other family members may range from fear to relief. The hospital environment may limit the types of interactions possible for the family.

In general, family members often feel that too much is happening too quickly. They may feel that they have too much to do and too little time. In view of both the ill person's changing physical status and the demands of day-to-day living, it is easy for family members to feel overwhelmed by the physical stresses inherent in the situation. Loss of sleep and inattention to good nutrition can contribute to the family's declining level of well-being. The physical health of all family members can become an almost ongoing concern in the therapeutic process.

Social Stresses

Few individuals or families receive sufficient social support when a loved one is dying. In the continuing process of obtaining and communicating accurate and current medical information within the family, communication patterns vary widely. Pre-existing patterns may become rigid during the crisis of death or grief. Often, past family conflicts are revived, such as sibling bitterness over the division of duties or the exclusion of certain family members in an exchange of confidences. Time-related pressures may lead to compulsive style behaviors. In an attempt to remain as functional as possible, families dealing with the crisis of death and grief often limit contact with helpful friends and social activities. Interventions at this time can have significant positive effects. Family members who may have been initially attentive sometimes withdraw in order to avoid painful situations, a very human response that may influence the family therapist.

Emotional Stresses

Even families with traditionally stable relationships may find their harmony severely threatened by the pressures associated with an impending death or grief over the recent death of a family member (Rosenbaum, 1978). The strain on family members can lead to a variety of emotional reactions, including anger, frustration, guilt, and feelings of desertion. These reactions produce physiological stress and emotional distress. The human homeostatic system can operate effectively only when environmental conditions remain within certain limits. Death of a loved one and the mourning response often overstretch the system. Situational and interpersonal changes disrupt affectional bonds and attachments, and separation becomes the major psychological and emotional concern. The greater that danger of loss appears, the more intense and varied the actions that are elicited to prevent it and to restore the bonds (Bowlby, 1980).

CHALLENGES TO THE FAMILY THERAPIST

Personal levels of anxiety and stress escalate at certain times. Therapists who work with families in the situations of death and grief must understand the major stressors in their work. A number of issues affect the amount or degrees of stress a family therapist experiences.

Expectations of Self or Client(s)

Medical care-givers are learning to look at the quality, not just the quantity, of a dying person's life. Just as physicians and nurses must redefine their roles as healers and become comforters when a person is dying, family therapists must also adjust their goals to focus on the individual as well as the family. Family therapists must understand that the goals and definitions for success in situations of impending death and recent bereavement can be very different from those in other circumstances. The dying process is rarely a tidy emotional experience (Lattanzi, 1981). Expecting individuals or families to follow a progression of stages that lead to a final magical state of acceptance only imposes rigid external standards on a highly personalized process. Family therapists need to approach dying individuals and grieving family members without attempting to control the process and without personally defining goals or success criteria for family members. The ambiguity that death creates is a significant stressor for all the individuals involved. Bias about a "right way" to die or a set view of the process simply creates further tension, as can be seen in the following example.

Mrs. Wilson called the hospice and requested family counseling. She and Mr. Wilson were in their early 50s and had been married less than 1 year. Mr. Wilson had lung cancer with extensive metastases and was deteriorating rapidly. He expressed an unwillingness to have hospice involvement in his care, although he very much wished to stay at home. Mrs. Wilson was employed full-time as a teacher. She had one 14-year-old daughter, Lisa, by a previous marriage. Mr. Wilson had four adult children, ranging in age from the middle 20s to the early 30s. Two sons, a daughter, a daughter-in-law, Lisa, Mrs. Wilson's sister, and Mrs. Wilson attended the initial meeting. Mrs. Wilson, who was exhausted, was trying to involve all the children in her husband's care. The children expressed various amounts of concern regarding Mr. Wilson's decision not to pursue further chemotherapy treatments. Mr. Wilson was also quite withdrawn at this point.

In the initial session, the varying needs of the children to have Mr. Wilson pursue more aggressive treatment became apparent. Mrs. Wilson had heard the physician's opinion that additional chemotherapy would not have a significant therapeutic effect. Each family member had an opinion on how Mr. Wilson should behave; conflicting desires among family members were clear. The goal that family members agreed on was to support Mr. Wilson's decisions related to care and treatment.

During the next 6 weeks, family members were able to experience some significant times with Mr. Wilson, even though his withdrawal continued. Subsequent sessions allowed family members to work on their conflicts, fears, and disagreements. There was no touching deathbed scene. Rather, family members supported Mr. Wilson's choices during his last weeks, no longer urging him to continue treatment. The family was not totally responsive to each other or cohesive, but the children were able to refocus their energy by increasing communication and involvement.

Family members and therapists can experience the highest levels of stress when they function on the basis of a rigid set of standards or beliefs related to the situation. Given support and permission to address their concerns, family members are usually able to function better and are generally less anxious.

Situational Limitations

Very often there are so many individuals in the therapeutic situation, bringing their past histories, that they crowd the environment emotionally. In many circumstances there can be too few individuals to help with the physical demands of caregiving. Also, when the person who is ill is hospitalized, the family must deal with a foreign environment, territorial issues, and a lack of privacy. The family therapist can help the family by offering transitional support and by exploring options during times of situational stress or crisis.

Time is often a situational stressor in that the demands related to work with these families can extend beyond the therapist's usual schedule. There are crises that need to be addressed immediately. Gwen Barbeè, a hospice nurse who had worked for over 5 years with families, reported that her greatest stress involved the feeling of never being off duty. Her involvement with a family as a key support person meant that she wanted to be present with the family when crises occurred. Like birth, death is not a pre-scheduled, preplanned event.

Proximity to Death

LaGrand (1980) related stress to forces on the job that make therapists feel inadequate. Death and grief are both powerful and often overpowering forces. The clients are vulnerable during these times, needing both perspective and information (Zelinski & Thorson, 1983); they are often seeking relief from an intolerable situation. Therapists who witness the suffering of others are changed. Realizing that little can be done about suffering, they change as a consequence of all suffering, their own as well as that of others (Kollar, 1982). Death's mysteriousness is a continuous reminder of our insignificance and transience. Lifton (1979) suggested that images are helpful in working with therapists' concerns. The image I have had in working with dying or grieving persons is one of standing near a fire. Clearly, the heat is intense, and one could get singed. The stress of care-giving is in experiencing the heat without running away and without getting burned.

Availability of Support

It is very difficult to work with dying or grieving persons alone. In order to manage their own stress, therapists who work with these families need a network of support that includes both work-related supports and personal support resources. Like the grieving families, however, few have sufficient support available or accessible in times of need. Bowlby (1980) pointed out that the response of others is a determining factor in how individuals manage the stress of loss. To a family therapist, a support network that includes a supervisor and colleagues who have a common language and understanding of experience is of immeasurable value, since therapy is intrinsically stressful for everyone. Parkes (1972) noted that everyone who confronts death needs a supportive environment nurtured by openness, compassion, and sensitive listening. The same support that therapists seek to offer families should be available to them as care-givers in a vulnerable situation.

Inner Resources

Helping professionals often ignore their own needs. Because they are used to being in a helping position, they may find it difficult to ask for support or even to acknowledge their own needs. To function well, however, therapists need successful experiences, outside supports, and a clear sense of their strengths and skills. Internal resources are as important as external support. The development and maintenance of these inner resources demand more attention and time when the work focuses on situations that are generally not defined in terms of success, such as work with dying persons and their families. Death itself, especially in a medical context, is seen as a failure.

In working with families after a death has occurred, therapeutic efforts are aimed at permitting feeling to emerge into consciousness. The task of learning to incorporate changes that result from the bereavement is not easily or rapidly accomplished. Progressively, family members realize the changes and establish a new set of assumptions about the world (Parkes, 1972). During the 1 to 2 years that this process can take, the rewards for a therapist are minimal. Family therapists who have had personal experiences with loss can use their direct knowledge as a sustaining influence. Success in working with dying or grieving persons is related to the therapist's ability to act as an advocate for the individual and the family (Lattanzi, 1981).

MANAGEMENT OF STRESS

Two important variables emerge in the management of stress: a therapist's life experience and communication of support. These variables also influence the way in which an individual copes with loss and eventually attempts to find some meaning from the experience. Therapists are definitely influenced by their past experiences, but a broad range of responses is possible in every situation. Communication and support allow therapists to adjust to the situational reality. Therapists who are highly defended cope by emotionally isolating themselves or by becoming standoffish. Some may adopt an attitude of intellectualized professionalism (Weisman, 1978). All the successful coping strategies are based on the situational reality. The behaviors that acknowledge and are congruent with experience can serve to deepen an individual's emotional life. Behaviors that avoid the situation eventually diminish an individual's sense of well-being. By modeling responses to a dying or bereaved person, therapists can present options for healthy responses.

It is possible to have too much direct contact with individuals or families as a helper. Time away from the work setting and the establishing of personal limits can reduce the impact of some stresses. In a hospice setting, policies often allow care-givers some respite time after a death occurs. Bereavement is a complex state, and it is seldom apparent exactly what was lost. In the eastern religious traditions, individuals are seen as mirrors, reflecting a picture of ourselves. When one of these mirrors is shattered or taken away, we operate for a period of time in an emotional deficit.

Therapists' View of Stress

Stress as a human experience requires almost constant attention and an ongoing adaptation. Therapists may believe that they have seen families at their worst during the crisis before death. Yet, the time of early, acute grief is another dysfunctional crisis time. Before and subsequent to the death, therapists can help families struggle with their sense of helplessness. Frustration, confusion, anger, and sorrow are all appropriate responses to loss. It seems important to look at families in these critical times as trying to reestablish homeostasis. There is a great need for information and acknowledgment of their personal experiences and the human responses to loss.

Past experiences and beliefs can strongly influence an individual's ability or perceived ability to manage grief.

A 50-year-old mother who had experienced the accidental deaths of two of her teen-aged sons in incidents 3½ years apart said that, having lived through the first intense grief process, she knew that she would somehow be able to live through this tragic loss, in spite of all her present pain.

It is difficult for therapists not to feel a sense of distress, outrage, and confusion over the injustices and tragedies that they witness. Our culture is heavily influenced by the Puritan beliefs that a "good life" keeps one safe from trauma and pain, and that tragedy is a form of punishment. These influences are subtle and unconscious, but they form the foundation for an individual's ability to cope with grief. As care-givers, therapists question the random nature of disease and accidents, however. It is difficult to accept the impending death of a 32-year-old woman; as her husband and children, aged 4 years and 2 months, struggle to function, professionals wrestle with their acute sense of powerlessness.

Our deepest beliefs and values are challenged by death's indiscriminate, unpredictable, and haunting presence. Like family members, therapists feel a deep and groundless uncertainty. This ambiguity changes across time as they witness the pain and courage of the human spirit during grief. Working with bereaved families is both difficult and inspiring. With awe, therapists watch bereaved parents reach out and offer support to more recently bereaved parents.

It is clear from the Holocaust experience that survival and resilience following great tragedy are related to the presence of support, as well as to an internal and personal framework of meaning. Frankl (1959) poignantly described how human beings can live through extreme stress and distress. Beyond his experience that survival is a collective act, Frankl wisely focused on human response to difficult circumstances as the only area in which humans have any control or power. Very often, care-givers wish for powers to change painful and tragic circumstances, but their only influence is in working with the family's response to their circumstance in supportive and compassionate ways. Work with families around issues of death and grief forces care-givers to face the limitations of their interventions.

Nouwen (1974) spoke of the caring that is needed when one is in a painful circumstance: "When we honestly ask ourselves which persons in our lives mean the most to us, we often find that it is those who instead of giving much advice, solutions, or cures have chosen rather to share our pain and touch our wounds with a gentle and tender hand." He went on to speak of the need for silence in times of despair or confusion and of the need for caring others to face their inability to know, cure, or heal—their powerlessness. A personal framework of beliefs that care-givers continue to examine and challenge is a powerful resource in the therapeutic relationship.

Coping Devices

Much has been written about the physical management of stress. Diet, exercise, and relaxation are all important to a sense of overall health. Stress must be addressed in all its components; emotional insight or meditation alone is not sufficient in the management of the physical manifestations of stress (Albrecht, 1982).

One widower could not find energy for any other activity but a long, brisk evening walk. Accompanied by his dog, the walk helped him keep occasional contact with neighbors. He also attributed his ability to sleep more regularly to the walks.

Physical wellness influences a person's total outlook on life and deserves primary attention.

The important dimension in the management of difficult circumstances is the ability to cope. Sheehy (1981) found that individuals with the highest levels of well-being turned most often to the following coping devices:

1. work more
2. depend on friends
3. see the humor in the situation
4. pray

She pointed out the recurring theme that people with high levels of well-being consistently relied on friends and associates for help. The most common responses found in people of low well-being were

1. drink more, eat more, take drugs—indulge
2. pretend the problem does not exist
3. develop physical symptoms
4. escape into fantasy

Family therapists can actively encourage the use of coping devices that lead to social support and creative adaptation.

PERSONAL REFLECTIONS

After years of working with people at painful times of their lives, I continue to be challenged to examine and explore the meaning of my own life. Frankl believed that work and relationships give our lives meaning. There is no question that, while working with individuals and families who are experiencing death and grief, I have been confronted with learnings that are profound and disquieting. It is difficult to feel the continuing presence of loss.

Worden (1982) noted the discomfort and fears that can be generated for counselors. It seems unlikely that we can rid ourselves or the families we work with of fears. Rather, acknowledging and facing our fears lead us to a greater potential for meaningful relationships and experiences. Garfield (1978) told of reading the phrase "the eternal silence of these infinite spaces frightens me" to a patient; the young man tearfully said that the phrase described why he was afraid. I, too, have been afraid when faced with the depths of pain, depths that in the moment appeared to be endless. The stress of facing pain somehow seems less than the cost of avoiding or repressing it, however.

Hospice workers often say that the rewards they receive are greater than the caring they give to others. Life is always a matter of timing and balance. The cost of doing this work can be offset by the rewards and the meaning it offers. This seems to be true for me in those times when I am experiencing the richness of my own life, without draining my resources by seeing too many clients and without racing the clock. In my experience, this is the most effective way to minimize work-related stresses. I will continue to ask myself whether it is in my best interest and in the best interest of the individuals and families I work with to continue in this field. This questioning is part of the challenge to live out the principles I attempt to encourage in families that I work with. By constantly developing my own personal awareness, I am learning and relearning Don Juan's understanding of the process of choosing to create my life:

[A]sk yourself and yourself alone one question. It is this: Does this path have a heart? All paths are the same. They lead nowhere. They are paths going through the brush or into the brush or under the brush. Does this path have a heart is the only question. If it does, then the path is good. If it doesn't, it is of no use. (Castaneda, 1974).

REFERENCES

Albrecht, T.L. What job stress means to the staff nurse. *Nursing Administration Quarterly,* 1982, 1–11.

Barbeé, Gwen. Personal communication, 1983.

Bowlby, J. *Attachment and loss, sadness and depression* (Vol. 3). New York: Basic Books, 1980.

Castaneda, C. *Journey to Ixtlan.* New York: Pocket Book, 1972.

Frankl, V.E. *Man's serach for meaning.* New York: Pocket Book, 1959.

Garfield, C.A. Introduction. In Garfield, C.A. (Ed.), *Psychosocial care of the dying patient.* New York: McGraw-Hill, 1978. (a)

Garfield, C.A. Elements of psychosocial oncology: Doctor-patient relationships in terminal illness. In C.A. Garfield (Ed.), *Psychosocial care of the dying patient.* New York: McGraw-Hill, 1978. (b)

Garfield, C.A. (Ed.), *Stress and survival.* St. Louis: C.V. Mosby, 1979.

Kollar, N. *Songs of suffering.* Minneapolis, MN: Winston Press, 1982.

Lattanzi, M.E. Coping with work-related losses. *Personnel and Guidance Journal,* 1981, 6(59), 350–51.

LaGrand, L.E. Reducing burnout in the hospice and the death education movement. *Death Education,* 1980, 4(1), 61–75.

Lifton, R.J. *The broken connection.* New York: Simon and Schuster, 1979.

Nouwen, H.J.M. *Out of solitude.* Notre Dame, IN: Ave Maria Press, 1974.

Parkes, C.M. *Bereavement: Studies of grief in adult life.* New York: International Universities Press, 1972.

Pattison, E.M. The living-dying process. In C.A. Garfield (Ed.), *Psychosocial care of the dying patient.* New York: McGraw-Hill, 1978.

Rosenbaum, E.H. Oncology/hematology and psychosocial support of the cancer patient. In C.A. Garfield (Ed.), *Psychosocial care of the dying patient.* New York: McGraw-Hill, 1978.

Sheehy, G. *Pathfinders.* New York: Wm. Morrow, 1981.

Weisman, A.D. Misgivings and misconceptions in the psychiatric care of terminal patients. In C.A. Garfield (Ed.), *Psychosocial care of the dying patient.* New York: McGraw-Hill, 1978.

Worden, J.W. *Grief counseling and grief therapy.* New York: Springer Publishing, 1982.

Zelinsky, L.F., & Thorson, J.A. Educational approaches to preparing social work students for practice related to death and dying. *Death Education,* 1983, (6)4.

Index to Collections 5-8

HOW TO USE THIS INDEX

The first number following the entry is the collection number: **5, 6, 7** or **8**. The number that follows is the page number within that collection where the reference will be found. For example, **5**/16-17 refers to Collection 5, pages 16 to 17.

Love, 5/8, 115
  romantic, 6/56
  unconditional, 8/6
  withdrawal of, 6/36-37
Lovisi v. Slayton, 5/166
Lower motor neuron injuries (LMN),
  5/140

Loyalty, 6/115
  children's, 5/120, 6/56
  cultural, 6/87, 117
  to family, 6/115
Lubrication-swelling response, 5/53-54
Lustful satisfaction, 5/36

M

McGoldrick, M., 7/102, 117
Machismo, 6/41-42
Mahler, M., 7/41-42
Make Today Count (support group),
  8/31, 32
Males
  aggressive, 6/41-42
  grieving process of, 8/17
  need of, to protect women, 5/121-122
  role of, 6/9-11
  sexual assault of, 5/110
  sexual response of, 5/138-139, 141,
    143
  See also Fathers
Malpractice suits, 5/158-159
Marital-Sexual Enrichment Program
  (Galveston), 5/55-59
Marriage
  deterioration of, 5/115, 6/62, 7/3, 7
  new, 5/21-22
  resolution of first, 7/106
  second, 7/107
  sex and, 5/10, 14
  and spousal rape, 5/110-112
  therapy of, 7/73, 76, 86

See also Family relationships;
  Partners; Remarriage families
Mastectomy, 5/143
Masturbation, 5/133-136, 141-142
"Mateship", 6/102
Matrilocal descent, 6/58
Meals on Wheels, 8/33
Mechanic, D., 8/76
Media, 5/38, 6/4
Mediators, 6/58
Medical examination, 5/116-117, 8/37
Medical Motor Service, 8/33
Medications. *See* Drugs
Melting pot myth, 6/12
Memory bank, imagistic, 5/16
Mental illness, 8/20, 24
  fear of, 8/20-21
  important loss and, 7/122
Metacode, 6/64
Metafamily, 7/101, 109
Metaphors, 6/143-144, 7/169
Mexican families, 6/58, 63, 69-72, 140
Microstructures, 7/20
Middle Eastern families, 6/17, 55
Migrant families, 6/37, 38, 131-132
Minuchin, S., 7/136
Mixed orientation couples, 5/83-85,
  87-88, 90-95
  See also Sexual orientation
Models (mannequins), child, 5/38
Mondanaro, Josette, 7/140
Monogamous family, 6/35
Morality, sexual, 5/33
Morphogenesis, 6/7
Morphostasis, 6/7
Mothers
  as head of household, 6/8-9
  loss of child by, 6/64-65, 8/2
  overprotection by, 6/41-42
  relationship of, with daughter, 5/125
  role of, in sexual abuse, 5/115
  role of, in abortion cases, 5/43
  traditional role of, 6/9-11
  working, 6/10-11